All These Things Added

JAMES ALLEN TITLES

All These Things Added

James Allen

MEDIA

Published 2019 by Gildan Media LLC
aka G&D Media
www.GandDmedia.com

Design by Meghan Day Healey of Story Horse, LLC

Library of Congress Cataloging-in-Publication Data is available upon request

ISBN: 978-1-7225-0248-5

10   9   8   7   6   5   4   3   2   1

Contents

Part I
ENTERING THE KINGDOM

Part II
THE HEAVENLY LIFE

Foreword

In seeking for pleasures here and rewards hereafter men have destroyed (in their hearts) the Temple of Righteousness, and have wandered from the Kingdom of Heaven. By ceasing to seek for earthly pleasures and heavenly rewards, the Temple of Righteousness is restored and the Kingdom of Heaven is found. This truth is for those who are ready to receive it; and this book also is for those whose souls have been prepared for the acceptance of its teaching.

—James Allen

Part I
ENTERING THE KINGDOM

The Soul's Great Need

I sought the world, but Peace was not there;
I courted learning, but Truth was not revealed;
I sojourned with philosophy, but my heart was
    sore with vanity.
And I cried, Where is Peace to be found!
And where is the hiding-place of Truth!
                –Filius Lucis

Every human soul is in need. The expression of that need varies with individuals, but there is not one soul that does not feel it in some degree. It is a spiritual and casual need which takes the form, in souls of a particular development, of a deep and inexpressible hunger which the outward things of life, however abundantly they may be possessed, can never satisfy. Yet the majority, imperfect in knowledge, and misled by appearances, seek to satisfy this hunger by striving for material possessions, believing that these will satisfy their need, and bring them peace.

Every soul, consciously or unconsciously, hungers for righteousness, and every soul seeks to gratify that hunger in its own particular way, and in accordance with its own particular state of knowledge. The hunger is one, and the righteousness is one, but the pathways by which righteousness is sought are many. They who seek consciously are blessed, and shall shortly find that final and permanent satisfaction of soul which righteousness alone can give, for they have come into a knowledge of the true path. They who seek unconsciously, although for a time they may bathe in a sea of pleasure, are not blessed, for they are carving out for themselves pathways of suffering over which they must walk with torn and wounded feet, and their hunger will increase, and the soul will cry out for its lost heritage—the eternal heritage of righteousness.

Not in any of the three worlds can the soul find lasting satisfaction, apart from the realization of righteousness. Bodied or disembodied, it is ceaselessly driven on by the discipline of suffering, until at last, in its extremity, it flies to its only refuge— the refuge of righteousness—and finds that joy, satisfaction, and peace which it had so long and so vainly sought.

The great need of the soul, then, is the need of this permanent principle, called righteousness, on which it may stand securely and restfully amid the tempest of earthly existence, no more bewildered, and whereon it may build the mansion of a beautiful, peaceful, and perfect life.

It is in the realization of this principle where the Kingdom of Heaven, the abiding home of the soul, resides, and which is the source and storehouse of every permanent blessing. Finding it, all is found; not finding it, all is lost. It is an attitude of mind, a state of consciousness, an ineffable knowledge, in which the struggle for existence ceases, and the soul finds itself at rest in the midst of plenty, where its great need, yea, its every need, is satisfied, without strife and without fear. Blessed are they who earnestly and intelligently seek, for it is impossible that such should seek in vain.

The Competitive Laws and the Law of Love

When I am pure
I shall have solved the mystery of life,
I shall be sure
(When I am free from hatred, lust and strife)
I am in Truth, and Truth abides in me.
I shall be safe and sane and wholly free
When I am pure.

It has been said that the laws of Nature are cruel; it has likewise been said that they are kind. The one statement is the result of dwelling exclusively upon the fiercely competitive aspect of Nature; the other results from viewing only the protective and kindly aspect. In reality, natural laws are neither cruel nor kind; they are absolutely just—are, in fact, the outworking of the indestructible principle of justice itself.

The cruelty, and consequent suffering, which is so prevalent in Nature, is not inherent in the heart and substance of life; it is a passing phase of evolution, a painful experience, which will ultimately ripen into the fruit of a more perfect knowledge; a dark night of ignorance and unrest, leading to a glorious morning of joy and peace.

When a helpless child is burnt to death, we do not ascribe cruelty to the working of the natural law by virtue of which the child was consumed; we infer ignorance in the child, or carelessness on the part of its guardians. Even so, men and creatures are daily being consumed in the invisible flames of passion, succumbing to the ceaseless interplay of those fiery psychic forces which, in their ignorance, they do not understand, but which they shall at last learn how to control and use to their own protection, and not, as at present, foolishly employ them to their own destruction.

To understand, control, and harmoniously adjust the invisible forces of its own soul is the ultimate destiny of every being and creature. Some men, in the past, have accomplished this supreme and exalted purpose; some, in the present, have likewise succeeded, and, until this is done, that place of rest wherein one receives all that is nec-

essary for one's well-being and happiness, without
striving, and with freedom from pain, cannot be
entered.

In an age like the present, when, in all civi-
lized countries, the string of life is strained to its
highest pitch, when men, striving each with each
in every department of life for the vanities and
material possessions of this perishable existence,
have developed competition to the utmost limit of
endurance—in such an age the sublimest heights
of knowledge are scaled, the supremest spiritual
conquests are achieved; for when the soul is most
tired, its need is greatest, and where the need is
great, great will be the effort. Where, also, the
temptations are powerful, the greater and more
enduring will be the victory. Men love the competitive strife with their fellows, while it promises, and
seems to bring them gain and happiness; but when
the inevitable reaction comes, and the cold steel of
selfish strife which their own hands have forged
enters their own hearts, then, and not till then,
do they seek a better way. "Blessed are they that
mourn"—that have come to the end of strife, and
have found the pain and sorrow to which it leads;
for unto them, and unto them only, can open the
door which leads to the Kingdom of Peace.

In searching for this Kingdom, it is necessary
to fully understand the nature and origin of that

which prevents its realization—namely, the strife of nature, the competitive laws operative in human affairs, and the universal unrest, insecurity, and fear which accompany these factors; for without such an understanding there can be no sound comprehension as to what constitutes the true and the false in life, and therefore no real spiritual advancement. Before the true can be apprehended and enjoyed, the false must be unveiled; before the real can be perceived as the real, the illusions which distort it must be dispersed; and before the limitless expanse of Truth can open out before us, the limited experience which is Confined to the world of visible and superficial effects must be transcended.

Let, therefore, those of my readers who are thoughtful and earnest, and who are diligently seeking, or are willing to seek, for that basis of thought and conduct which shall simplify and harmonize the bewildering complexities and inequalities of life, walk with me step by step as I open up the way to the Kingdom; first descending into Hell (the world of strife and self-seeking) in order that, having comprehended its intricate ways, we may afterwards ascend into Heaven (the world of Peace and Love).

It is the custom in my household, during the hard frosts of winter, to put out food for the birds, and it is a noticeable fact that these creatures, when they are really starving, live together most amicably, huddling together to keep each other warm, and refraining from all strife; and if a small quantity of food be given them they will eat it with comparative freedom from contention; but let a quantity of food which is more than sufficient for all be thrown to them, and fighting over the coveted provender at once ensues. Occasionally we would put out a whole loaf of bread, and then the contention of the birds became fierce and prolonged, although there was more than they all could possibly eat during several days. Some, having gorged themselves until they could eat no more, would stand upon the loaf and hover round it, pecking fiercely at all newcomers, and endeavoring to prevent them from obtaining any of the food. And along with this fierce contention there was noticeable a great fear. With each mouthful of food taken, the birds would look round in nervous terror, apprehensive of losing their food or their lives.

In this simple incident we have an illustration—crude, perhaps, but true—of the basis and outworking of the competitive laws in Nature and in human affairs. It is not scarcity that produces competition, *it is abundance*; so that the richer and more luxurious a nation becomes, the keener and fiercer becomes the competition for securing the

necessaries and luxuries of life. Let famine overtake a nation, and at once compassion and sym-
pathy take the place of competitive strife; and, in
the blessedness of giving and receiving, men enjoy
a foretaste of that heavenly bliss which the spiritually wise have found, and which all shall ultimately reach.

The fact that abundance, and not scarcity,
creates competition, should be held constantly
in mind by the reader during the perusal of this
book, as it throws a searching light not only on the
statements herein contained, but upon every problem relating to social life and human conduct.

Moreover, if it be deeply and earnestly medi-
tated upon, and its lessons applied to individual
conduct, it will make plain the Way which leads to
the Kingdom.

Let us now search out the *cause* of this fact, in
order that the evils connected with it may be transcended.

Every phenomenon in social and national life
(as in Nature) is an effect, and all these effects are
embodied by a cause which is not remote and
detached, but which is the immediate soul and life
of the effect itself. As the seed is contained in the
flower, and the flower in the seed, so the relation
of cause and effect is intimate and inseparable. An
effect, also, is vivified and propagated, not by any

life inherent in itself, but by the life and impulse existing in the cause.

Looking out upon the world, we behold it as an arena of strife in which individuals, communities, and nations are constantly engaged in struggle, striving with each other for superiority, and for the largest share of worldly possessions. We see, also, that the weaker fall out defeated, and that the strong—those who are equipped to pursue the combat with undiminished ardor—obtain the victory, and enter into possession. And along with this struggle we see the suffering which is inevitably connected with it—men and women, broken down with the weight of their responsibilities, failing in their efforts and losing all; families and communities broken up, and nations subdued and subordinated. We see seas of tears, telling of unspeakable anguish and grief; we see painful partings and early and unnatural deaths; and we know that this life of strife, when stripped of its surface appearances, is largely a life of sorrow.

Such, briefly sketched, are the phenomena connected with that aspect of human life with which we are now dealing; such are the effects as we see them; and they have one common cause which is found in the human heart itself. As all the multiform varieties of plant life have one common soil from which to draw their sustenance, and by virtue of which they live and thrive, so all the varied activities of human life are rooted in, and draw their vitality from, one common source—*the human heart*. The cause of all suffering and of all happiness resides, not in the outer activities of human life, but in the inner activities of the heart and mind; and every external agency is sustained by the life which it derives from human conduct.

The organized life-principle in man carves for itself outward channels along which it can pour its pent-up energies, makes for itself vehicles through which it can manifest its potency and reap its experience, and, as a result, we have our religious, social, and political organizations.

All the visible manifestations of human life, then, are effects; and as such, although they may possess a reflex action, they can never be causes, but must remain forever what they are—*dead effects*, galvanized into life by an enduring and profound cause.

It is the custom of men to wander about in this world of effects, and to mistake its illusions for realities, eternally transposing and readjusting these effects in order to arrive at a solution of human problems, instead of reaching down to the underlying cause which is at once the center of unification and the basis upon which to build a peace-giving solution of human life.

The strife of the world in all its forms, whether it be war, social or political quarreling, sectarian hatred, private disputes, or commercial competition, has its origin in one common cause, namely, *individual selfishness.* And I employ this term selfishness in a far-reaching sense; in it I include all forms of self-love and egotism—I mean by it the desire to pander to, and preserve at all costs, the personality.

This element of selfishness is the life and soul of competition, and of the competitive laws. Apart from it they have no existence. But in the life of every individual in whose heart selfishness in any form is harbored, these laws are brought into play, and the individual is subject to them.

Innumerable economic systems have failed, and must fail, to extirpate the strife of the world. They are the outcome of the delusion that outward systems of government are the causes of that strife, whereas they are but the visible and transient effect of the *inward strife,* the channels through which it must necessarily manifest itself. To destroy the channel is, and must ever be, ineffectual, as the inward energy will immediately make for itself another, and still another and another. Strife cannot cease; and the competitive laws *must prevail so long as selfishness is fostered in the heart.* All reforms will fail where this element is ignored or unaccounted for; all reforms will succeed where it is recognized, and steps are taken for its removal.

Selfishness, then, is the root cause of competition, the foundation on which all competitive systems rest, and the sustaining source of the competitive laws. It will thus be seen that all competitive systems, all the visible activities of the struggle of man with man, are as the leaves and branches of a tree which overspreads the whole earth, the root of that tree being *individual selfishness*, and the ripened fruits of which are pain and sorrow. This tree cannot be destroyed by merely lopping off its branches; to do this effectually, *the root must be destroyed*. To introduce measures in the form of changed external conditions is merely lopping off the branches; and as the cutting away of certain branches of a tree gives added vigor to those which remain, even so the very means which are taken to curtail the competitive strife, when those means deal entirely with its outward effects, will but add strength and vigor to the tree whose roots are all the time being fostered and encouraged in the human heart. The most that even legislation can do is to prune the branches, and so prevent the tree from altogether running wild.

Great efforts are now being put forward to found a "Garden City," which shall be a veritable Eden planted in the midst of orchards, and whose inhabitants shall live in comfort and comparative repose. And beautiful and laudable are all such efforts when they are prompted by unselfish love. But such a city cannot exist, or cannot long remain the Eden which it aims to be in its outward form, unless the majority of its inhabitants have subdued and conquered the inward selfishness. Even one form of selfishness, namely, *self-indulgence*, if fostered by its inhabitants, will completely undermine that city, leveling its orchards to the ground, converting many of its beautiful dwellings into competitive marts, and obnoxious centers for the personal gratification of appetite, and some of its public buildings into institutions for the maintenance of order; and upon its public spaces will rise jails, asylums, and orphanages, for where the spirit of self-indulgence is, the means for its gratification will be immediately adopted, without considering the good of others or of the community (for selfishness is always blind), and the fruits of that gratification will be rapidly reaped.

The building of pleasant houses and the planting of beautiful orchards and gardens can never, of itself, constitute a Garden City unless its inhabitants have learned that self-sacrifice is better than self-protection, and have first established in their own hearts the Garden City of unselfish love. And when a sufficient number of men and women have done this, the Garden City will appear, and it will flourish and prosper, and great will be its peace, for "out of the heart are the issues of life."

Having found that selfishness is the root cause of all competition and strife, the question naturally arises as to how this cause shall be dealt with, for it naturally follows that a cause being destroyed, all its effects cease; a cause being propagated, all its effects, however they may be modified from without, *must* continue. Every man who has thought at all deeply upon the problem of life, and has brooded sympathetically upon the sufferings of mankind, has seen that selfishness is at the root of all sorrow—in fact, this is one of the truths that is first apprehended by the thoughtful mind. And along with that perception there has been born within him a longing to formulate some methods by which that selfishness might be overcome. The first impulse of such a man is to endeavor to frame some outward law, or introduce some new social arrangements or regulations, which shall put a check on *the selfishness of others*. The second tendency of his mind will be to feel his utter helplessness before the great iron wall of selfishness by which he is confronted. Both these attitudes of mind are the result of an incomplete knowledge of what constitutes selfishness. And this partial knowledge dominates him because, although he has overcome the grosser forms of selfishness in himself, and is so far noble, he is yet selfish in other and more remote and subtle directions. This feeling of "helplessness" is the prelude to one of two conditions—the man will either give up in despair, and again sink himself in the selfishness of the world, or he will search and meditate until he finds another way out of the difficulty. And that way he will find. Looking deeper and ever deeper into the things of life; reflecting, brooding, examining, and analyzing; grappling with every difficulty and problem with intensity of thought, and developing day by day a profounder love of Truth—by these means his heart will grow and his comprehension expand, and at last he will realize that the way to destroy selfishness is not to try to destroy *one form* of it in other people, but to destroy it utterly, root and branch, *in himself.*

The perception of this truth constitutes spiritual illumination, and when once it is awakened in the mind, the "straight and narrow way" is revealed, and the shining Gates of the Kingdom already loom in the distance. Then does a man apply to himself (not to others) these words—"And why beholdest thou the mote that is in thy brother's eye, but considerest not the beam that is in thine own eye? Or how wilt thou say to thy brother, let me pull out the mote out of thine eye; and, behold, a beam is in thine own eye? Thou hypocrite, first cast out the beam out of thine own eye; and then shalt thou see clearly to cast out the mote out of thy brother's eye." When a man can apply these words to himself and act upon them, judging himself mercilessly, but judging none other, then will he find his way out of the hell of competitive strife, then will he rise above and render of non-effect the laws of competition, and will find the higher Law of Love, subjecting himself to which every evil thing will flee from him, and the joys and blessings which the selfish vainly seek will constantly wait upon him. And not only this, he will, having lifted himself, lift the world. By his example many will see the Way, and will walk it; and the powers of darkness will be the weaker for his having lived.

It will here be asked, "But will not a man who has risen above his selfishness, and therefore above the competitive strife, suffer through the selfishness and competition of those around him? Will he not, after all the trouble he has taken to purify himself, suffer at the hands of the impure?" No, he will not. The equity of the Divine Order is perfect, and cannot be subverted, so that it is impossible for one who has overcome selfishness to be subject to those laws which are brought into operation by the action of selfishness; in other words, each individual suffers by virtue of his own selfishness.

It is true that the selfish all come under the operation of the competitive laws, and suffer collec-
tively, each acting, more or less, as the instrument
by which the suffering of others is brought about,
which makes it appear, on the surface, as though
men suffered for the sins of others rather than their
own. But the truth is that in a universe the very
basis of which is harmony, and which can only be
sustained by the perfect adjustment of all its parts,
each unit receives *its own* measure of adjustment,
and suffers by and of itself. Each man comes under
the laws of his own being, never under those of
another. True, he will suffer like another, and even
through the instrumentality of another, if he elects
to live under the same conditions as that other.
But if he chooses to desert those conditions and to
live under another and higher set of conditions of
which that other is ignorant, he will cease to come
under, or be affected by, the lower laws.

Let us now go back to the symbol of the tree,
and carry the analogy a little further. Just as the
leaves and branches are sustained by the roots, so
the roots derive their nourishment from the soil,
groping blindly in the darkness for the sustenance
which the tree demands. In like manner, selfishness, the root of the tree of evil and of suffering,
derives its nourishment from the dark soil of *ignorance*. In this it thrives; upon this it stands and

flourishes. By ignorance I mean something vastly different from lack of learning; and the sense in which I use it will be made plain as I proceed.

Selfishness always gropes in the dark. It has no knowledge; by its very nature it is cut off from the source of enlightenment; it is a blind impulse, knowing nothing, obeying no law, for it knows none, and is thereby forcibly bound to those competitive laws by virtue of which suffering is inflicted in order that harmony may be maintained. We live in a world, a universe, abounding with all good things. So great is the abundance of spiritual, mental, and material blessings that every man and woman on this globe could not only be provided with every necessary good, but could live in the midst of abounding plenty, and yet leave much to spare. Yet, in spite of this, what a spectacle of ignorance do we behold! We see on the one hand millions of men and women chained to a ceaseless slavery, interminably toiling in order to obtain a poor and scanty meal and a garment to cover their nakedness; and on the other hand we see thousands, who already have more than they require and can well manage, depriving themselves of all the blessings of a true life and of the vast opportunities which their possessions place within their reach, in order to accumulate more of those material things for which they have no legitimate use.

Surely men and women have no more wisdom than the beasts which fight over the possession of that which is more than they can all well dispose of, and which they could all enjoy in peace!

Such a condition of things can only obtain in a state of ignorance deep and dark; so dark and dense as to be utterly impenetrable save to the unselfish eye of wisdom and truth. And in the midst of all this striving after place and food and raiment, there works unseen, yet potent and unerring, the Over-ruling Law of Justice, meting out to every individual his own quota of merit and demerit.

It is impartial; it bestows no favors; it inflicts no unearned punishments:

It knows not wrath nor pardon; utter-true
  It measures mete, its faultless balance weighs;
Times are as nought, tomorrow it will judge,
  Or after many days.

The rich and the poor alike suffer for *their own selfishness*; and none escapes. The rich have their particular sufferings as well as the poor. Moreover, the rich are continually losing their riches; the poor are continually acquiring them. The poor man of today is the rich man of tomorrow, and *vice versa*. There is no stability, no security in hell, and only brief and occasional periods of respite from suffering in some form or other. Fear, also, follows men like a great shadow, for the man who obtains and holds by selfish force will always be haunted by a feeling of insecurity, and will continually fear its loss; while the poor man, who is selfishly seeking or coveting material riches, will be harassed by the fear of destitution. And one and all who live in this underworld of strife are overshadowed by one great fear—the fear of death.

Surrounded by the darkness of ignorance, and having no knowledge of those eternal and life-sustaining Principles out of which all things proceed, men labor under the delusion that the most important and essential things in life are food and clothing, and that their first duty is to strive to obtain these, believing that these outward things are the source and cause of all comfort and happiness. It is the blind animal instinct of self-preservation (the preservation of the body and personality), by virtue of which each man opposes himself to other men in order to "get a living" or "secure a competency," believing that if he does not keep an incessant watch on other men, and constantly renew the struggle, they will ultimately "take the bread out of his mouth."

It is out of this initial delusion that comes all the train of delusions, with their attendant sufferings, which obtain in the world around us. Food and clothing are not the *essential* things of life; not the causes of happiness. They are non-essentials, effects, and, as such, proceed by a process of natural law from the essentials, the underlying cause. The essential things in life are the enduring elements in character—integrity, faith, righteousness, self-sacrifice, compassion, love; and out of these all good things proceed. Food, clothing, and money are dead effects; there is in them no life, no power except that with which we invest them. They are without vice and virtue, and can neither bless nor harm. Even the body which men believe to be themselves, to which they pander, and which they long to keep, must very shortly be yielded up to the dust. But the higher elements of character are life itself; and to practice these, to trust them, and to live entirely in them, constitutes the Kingdom of Heaven.

The man who says, "I will first of all earn a competence and secure a good position in life, and will then give my mind to these higher things," does not understand these higher things, does not believe them to be higher, for if he did, it would not be possible for him to neglect them. He believes the material excrescences of life to be the higher, and therefore he seeks them first. He believes money, clothing, and position to be of vast and essential importance, righteousness and truth to be at best secondary; for a man always sacrifices that which he believes to be lesser to that which he believes to be greater. Immediately a man *realizes* that righteousness is of more importance than the getting of food and clothing, he ceases to strive after the latter, and begins to live for the former. It is here where we come to the dividing line between the two Kingdoms—Hell and Heaven.

Once a man perceives the beauty and enduring reality of righteousness, his whole attitude of mind toward himself and others and the things within and around him changes. The love of personal existence gradually loses its hold on him; the instinct of self-preservation begins to die, and the practice of self-renunciation takes its place. For the sacrifice of others, or of the happiness of others, for his own good, he substitutes the sacrifice of self and of his own happiness for the good of others. And thus, rising above self, he rises above the competitive strife which is the outcome of self, and above the competitive laws which operate only in the region of self, and for the regulation of its blind impulses. He is like a man who has climbed a mountain, and thereby risen above all the disturbing currents in the valleys below him. The clouds pour down their rain, the thunders roll and the lightnings flash, the fogs obscure, and the hurricanes uproot and destroy, but they cannot reach him on the calm heights where he stands, and where he dwells in continual sunshine and peace.

In the life of such a man the lower laws cease to operate, and he now comes under the protection of a higher Law—namely, the Law of Love; and, in accordance with his faithfulness and obedience to this Law, will all that is necessary for his well-being come to him at the time when he requires it. The idea of gaining a position in the world cannot enter his mind, and the external necessities of life, such as money, food, and clothing, he scarcely ever thinks about. But, subjecting himself for the good of others, performing all his duties scrupulously and without thinking of reward, and living day by day in the discipline of righteousness, all other things follow at the right time and in the right order. Just as suffering and strife inhere in, and spring from, their root cause, selfishness, so blessedness and peace inhere in, and spring from, their root cause, righteousness. And it is a full and all-embracing blessedness, complete and perfect in every department of life, for that which is morally and spiritually right is physically and materially right.

Such a man is free, for he is freed from all anxiety, worry, fear, despondency, all those mental disturbances which derive their vitality from the elements of self, and he lives in constant joy and peace, and this while living in the very midst of the competitive strife of the world. Yet, though walking in the midst of Hell, its flames fall back before and around him, so that not one hair of his head can be singed. Though he walks in the midst of the lions of selfish force, for him their jaws are closed and their ferocity is subdued. Though on every hand men are falling around him in the fierce battle of life, he falls not, neither is he dismayed, for no deadly bullet can reach him, no poisoned shaft can pierce the impenetrable armor of his righteousness. Having lost the little, personal, self-seeking life of suffering, anxiety, fear, and want, he has found the illimitable, glorious, self-perfecting life of joy and peace and plenty. "Therefore take no thought, saying, What shall we eat? or, What shall we drink? or, Wherewithal shall we be clothed? . . . For your heavenly Father knoweth ye have need of all these things. But seek ye first the Kingdom of God, and His Righteousness; and all these things shall be added unto you."

The Finding
of a Principle

Be still, my soul, and know that peace is thine.
Be steadfast, heart, and know that strength
divine
Belongs to thee; cease from thy turmoil, mind,
And thou the everlasting rest shalt find.

How then shall a man reach the Kingdom? By
what process shall he find the light which
alone can disperse his darkness? And in what
way can he overcome the inward selfishness which
is strong, and deeply rooted?

A man will reach the Kingdom by purifying
himself, and he can only do this by pursuing a
process of self-examination and self-analysis. The
selfishness must be discovered and understood
before it can be removed. It is powerless to remove
itself, neither will it pass away of itself. Darkness

ceases only when light is introduced; so ignorance can only be dispersed by Knowledge; selfishness by Love. Seeing that in selfishness there is no security, no stability, no peace, the whole process of seeking the Kingdom resolves itself into a search for a Principle; a divine and permanent Principle on which a man can stand secure, freed from himself—that is, from the personal element, and from the tyranny and slavery which that personal self exacts and demands. A man must first of all be willing to lose himself (his self-seeking self) before he can find himself (his divine self). He must realize that selfishness is not worth clinging to, that it is a master altogether unworthy of his service, and that divine Goodness alone is worthy to be enthroned in his heart as the supreme master of his life. This means that he must have faith, for without this equipment there can be neither progress nor achievement. He must believe in the desirability of purity, in the supremacy of righteousness, in the sustaining power of integrity; he must ever hold before him the Ideal and Perfect Goodness, and strive for its achievement with ever-renewed effort and unflagging zeal. This faith must be nurtured and its development encouraged. As a lamp, it must be carefully trimmed and fed and kept burning in the heart, for without its radiating flame no way will be seen in the darkness; he will find no pathway out of self. And as this flame increases and burns with a steadier light, energy, resolution, and self-reliance will come to his aid, and with each step, his progress will be accelerated until at last the Light of Knowledge will begin to take the place of the lamp of faith, and the darkness will commence to disappear before its searching splendor. Into his spiritual ken will come the Principles of the divine Life, and as he approaches them, their incomparable beauty and majestic symmetry will astonish his vision, and gladden his heart with a gladness hitherto unknown.

Along this pathway of self-control and self-purification (for such it is) every soul must travel on its way to the Kingdom. So narrow is this way, and so overgrown with the weeds of selfishness is its entrance, that it is difficult to find, and, being found, cannot be retained except by *daily meditation*. Without this the spiritual energies grow weaker, and the man loses the strength necessary to continue. As the body is sustained and invigorated by material food, so the spirit is strengthened and renewed by its own food—namely, meditation upon spiritual things.

He, then, who earnestly resolves to find the Kingdom will commence to meditate, and to rigidly examine his heart and mind and life in the light of that Supreme Perfection which is the goal of his attainment. On his way to that goal, he must pass through *three Gateways of Surrender.* The first is *the Surrender of Desire*; the second is *the Surrender of Opinion*; the third is *the Surrender of Self.* Entering into meditation, he will commence to examine his desires, tracing them out in his mind, and following up their effects in his life and upon his character; and he will quickly perceive that, without the renunciation of desire, a man remains a slave both to himself and to his surroundings and circumstances. Having discovered this, the first Gate, that of *the Surrender of Desire*, is entered. Passing through this Gate, he adopts a process of self-discipline which is the first step in the purification of the soul. Hitherto he has lived as a slavish beast; eating, drinking, sleeping, and pursuing enjoyment at the beck and call of his lower impulses; blindly following and gratifying his inclinations without method, not questioning his conduct, and having no fixed center from which to regulate his character and life. Now, however, he begins to live as a man; he curbs his inclinations, controls his passions, and steadies his mind in the practice of virtue. He ceases to pursue enjoyment, but follows the dictates of his reason, and regulates his conduct in accordance with the demands of an ideal. With the introduction of this regulating factor in his life, he at once perceives that certain habits must be abandoned. He begins to select his food, and to have his meals at stated periods, no longer eating at any time when the sight of food tempts his inclination. He reduces the number of meals per day and also the quantity of food eaten. He no longer goes to bed, by day or night, to indulge in pleasurable indolence, but to give his body the rest it needs, and he therefore regulates his hours of sleep, rising early, and never encouraging the animal desire to indulge in dreamy indolence after waking. All those foods and drinks which are particularly associated with gluttony, cruelty, and drunkenness he will dispense with altogether, selecting the mild and refreshing sustenance which Nature provides in such rich profusion.

These preliminary steps will be at once adopted; and as the path of self-government and self-examination is pursued, a clearer and ever clearer perception of the nature, meaning, and effects of desire will be developed, until it will be seen that the mere regulation of one's desires is altogether inadequate and insufficient, and that *the desires themselves must be abandoned*, must be allowed to fall out of the mind and to have no part in the character and life. It is at this point where the soul of the seeker will enter the dark Valley of Temptation, for these desires will not die without a struggle, and without many a fierce effort to reassert the power and authority with which they have hitherto been invested. And here the lamp of faith must be constantly fed and assiduously trimmed, for all the light that it can throw out will be required to guide and encourage the traveler in the dense gloom of this dark Valley. At first his desires, like so many wild beasts, will clamor loudly for gratification. Failing in that, they will then tempt him to struggle with them that they may overthrow him. And this last temptation is greater and more difficult to overcome than the first, for *the desires will not be stilled until they are utterly ignored*; until they are left unheeded, unconditionally abandoned, and allowed to perish for want of food. In passing through this Valley, the searcher will develop certain powers which are necessary to his further advancement, and these powers are—*self-control, self-reliance, fearlessness*, and *independence of thought.* Here also he will have to pass through ridicule and mockery and false accusation; so much so that some of his best friends, yea, even those whom he most unselfishly loves, will accuse him of folly and inconsistency, and will do all they can to argue him back to the life of animal indulgence, self-seeking, and petty personal strife. Nearly everybody around him will suddenly discover that they know his duty better than he knows it himself, and, knowing no other and higher life than their own of mingled excitement and suffering, they will take great pains to win him back to it, imagining, in their ignorance, that he is losing so much pleasure and happiness, and is gaining nothing in return. At first this attitude of others toward him will arouse in him acute suffering, but he will rapidly discover that this suffering is caused by his own vanity and selfishness, and is the result of his own subtle desire to be appreciated, admired, and thought well of; and immediately this knowledge is arrived at, he will rise into a higher state of consciousness, where these things can no longer reach him and inflict pain. It is here where he will begin to stand firm, and to wield with effect the powers of mind already mentioned. Let him therefore press on courageously, heeding neither the revilings of his friends without nor the clamorings of his enemies within; aspiring, searching, striving; looking ever toward his Ideal with eyes of holy love; day by day ridding his mind of selfish motive, his heart of impure desire; stumbling sometimes, sometimes falling, but ever traveling onward and rising higher; and, recording each night in the silence of his own heart the journey of the day, let him not despair if but each day, in spite of all its failures and falls, record some holy battle fought, though lost, some silent victory attempted, though unachieved. The loss of today will add to the gain

of tomorrow for him whose mind is set on the conquest of self.

Passing along the Valley, he will at last come to
the Fields of Sorrow and Loneliness. His desires,
having received at his hands neither encourage-
ment nor sustenance, have grown weak, and are
now falling away and perishing. He is now climb-
ing out of the Valley, and the darkness is less
dense; but now he realizes, for the first time, that
he is alone. He is like a man standing upon the
lowest level of a great mountain, and it is night.
Above him towers the lofty peak, beyond which
shine the everlasting stars; a short distance below
him are the glaring lights of the city which he has
left, and from it there come up to him the noises
of its inhabitants—a confused mingling of shouts,
screams, laughter, rumblings of traffic, and the
strains of music. He thinks of his friends, all of
whom are in the city, pursuing their own particular pleasures, and he is alone upon the mountain.
That city is the City of Desire and Pleasure, the
mountain is the Mountain of Renunciation, and
the climber now knows that he has left the world,
that henceforth for him its excitements and strifes
are lifeless things, and can tempt him no more.
Resting awhile in this lonely place, he will taste of
sorrow and learn its secret; harshness and hatred
will pass from him; his heart will grow soft, and

the first faint broodings of that divine compassion, which shall afterwards absorb his whole being, will overshadow and inspire him. He will begin to feel with every living thing in its strivings and sufferings, and gradually, as this lesson is learned, his own sorrow and loneliness will be forgotten in his great calm love for others, and will pass away.

Here, also, he will begin to perceive and understand the working of those hidden laws which govern the destinies of individuals and nations. Having risen above the lower region of strife and selfishness within himself, he can now look calmly down upon it in others and in the world, and analyze and comprehend it, and he will see how selfish striving is at the root of all the world's suffering. His whole attitude toward others and the world now undergoes a complete change, and compassion and love begin to take the place of self-seeking and self-protection in his mind; and as a result of this, the world alters in its attitude toward him. At this juncture he perceives the folly of competition, and, ceasing from striving to overtop and get the better of others, he begins to encourage them, both with unselfish thoughts, and, when necessary, with loving acts; and this he does even to those who selfishly compete with him, no longer defending himself against them. As a direct result of this, his worldly affairs begin to prosper as never before; many of the friends who at first mocked him commence to respect, and even to love him, and he suddenly wakes up to the fact that he is coming in contact with people of a distinctly unworldly and noble type, of whose existence he had no knowledge while living in his lower selfish nature. From many parts and from long distances these people will come to him to minister to him and that he may minister to them, spiritual fellowship and loving brotherhood will become potent factors in his life, and so he will pass beyond the Fields of Sorrow and Loneliness.

The lower competitive laws have now ceased to operate in his life, and their results, which are *failure, disaster, exposure,* and *destitution*, can no longer enter into and form part of his experience; and this not merely because he has risen above the lower forms of selfishness in himself, but because also, in so rising, he has developed certain power of mind by which he is enabled to direct and govern his affairs with a more powerful and masterly hand.

He, however, has not yet traveled far, and unless he exercise constant watchfulness, may at any time fall back into the lower world of darkness and strife, revivifying its empty pleasures, and galvanizing back to life its dead desires. And especially is there this danger when he reaches the greatest temptation through which man is called to pass—*the temptation of doubt*. Before reaching, or even perceiving, the second Gate, that of *Surrender of Opinion*, the pilgrim will come upon a great soul-desert, the Desert of Doubt. And here for a time he will wander around, and despondency, indecision, and uncertainty, a melancholy brood, will surround him like a cloud, hiding from his view the way immediately in front of him. A new and strange fear, too, will possibly overtake him, and he will begin to question the wisdom of the course he is pursuing. Again the allurements of the world will be presented to him, dressed in their most attractive garb, and the drowning din and stimulating excitement of worldly battle will once more assume a desirable aspect. "After all, am I right?" "What gain is there in this?" "Does not life itself consist of pleasure and excitement and battle, and in giving these up am I not giving up all?" "Am I not sacrificing the very substance of life for a meaningless shadow?" "May it not be that, after all, I am a poor deluded fool, and that all these around me who live the life of the senses and stand upon its solid, sure, and easily procured enjoyments are wiser than I?" By such dark doubtings and questionings will he here be tempted and troubled, and these very doubts will drive him to a deeper searching into the intricacies of life, and arouse within him the feeling of necessity for some permanent Principle upon which to stand and take refuge. He will therefore, while wandering about in this dark Desert, come into contact with the higher and more subtle delusions of his own mind, the delusions of the intellect; and, by contrasting these with his Ideal, will learn to distinguish between the real and the unreal, the shadow and the substance, between effect and cause, between fleeting appearances and permanent Principles.

In the Desert of Doubt a man is confronted with all forms of illusion, not only the illusions of the senses, but also those of abstract thought and religious emotion. It is in the testing of, grappling with, and ultimately destroying these illusions that he develops still higher powers, those of *discrimination, spiritual perception, steadfastness of purpose,* and *calmness of mind,* by the exercise of which he is enabled to unerringly distinguish the true from the false, both in the world of thought and that of material appearances. Having acquired these powers, and learned how to use them in his holy warfare as weapons against himself, he now emerges from the Desert of Doubt, the mists and mirages of delusion vanish from his pathway, and there looms before him the second Gate, the *Gateway of the Surrender of Opinion.*

As he approaches this Gate, he sees before him the whole pathway along which he is traveling, and, for a space, obtains a glimpse of the glorious heights of attainment toward which he is moving; he sees the Temple of the Higher Life in all its majesty, and already he feels within him the strength and joy and peace of conquest. With Sir Galahad he can now exclaim:

> *I . . . saw the Grail,*
> *The Holy Grail . . .*
> *. . . And one will crown me king*
> *Far in the spiritual city,*

for he knows that his ultimate victory is assured.

He now enters upon a process of self-conquest, which is altogether distinct from that which he has hitherto pursued. Up to the present he has been overcoming, transmuting, and simplifying his animal desires; now he commences to transmute and simplify his intellect. He has, so far, been adjusting his *feelings* to his Ideals; he now begins to adjust his *thoughts* to that Ideal, which also assumes at this point larger and more beautiful proportions, and for the first time he perceives what really constitutes *a permanent and imperishable Principle*. He sees that the righteousness for which he has been searching is fixed and unvariable; that it cannot be accommodated to man, but that man must reach up to, and obey it; that it consists of an undeviating line of conduct, apart from all considerations of loss or gain, of reward or punishment; that, in reality, it consists in abandoning self, with all the sins of desire, opinion, and self-interest of which that self is composed, and in living the blameless life of perfect love toward all men and creatures. Such a life is fixed and perfect; it is without turning, change, or qualification, and demands a sinless and perfect conduct. It is, therefore, the direct antithesis of the worldly life of self.

Perceiving this, the seeker sees that, although he has freed himself from the baser passions and desires which enslave mankind, he is still in bondage to the fetters of opinion; that although he has purified himself with a purity to which few aspire, and which the world cannot understand, he is still defiled with a defilement which is difficult to wash away—*he loves his own opinions*, and has all along been confounding them with Truth, with the Principle for which he is seeking. He is not yet free from strife, and is still involved in the competitive laws as they obtain in the higher realm of thought. He still believes that he (in his opinions) is right, and that others are wrong; and, in his egotism, has even fallen so low as to bestow a mock pity on those who hold opinions the reverse of his own. But now, realizing this more subtle form of selfishness with which he is enslaved, and perceiving all the train of sufferings which spring from it, having also acquired the priceless possession of spiritual discernment, he reverently bends his head and passes through the second Gateway toward his final peace.

And now, clothing his soul with the colorless Garment of Humility, he bends all his energies to the uprooting of those opinions which he has hitherto loved and cherished. He now learns to distinguish between Truth, which is one and unchangeable, and his own and others' opinions about Truth, which are many and changeable. He sees that his *opinions* about Goodness, Purity, Compassion, and Love are very distinct from those qualities themselves, and that he must stand upon those divine Principles, and not upon his opinions. Hitherto he has regarded his own opinions as of great value, and the opinions of others as worthless, but now he ceases to so elevate his own opinions and to defend them against those of others, and comes to regard them as utterly worthless. As a direct result of this attitude of mind, he takes refuge in the practice of *pure Goodness*, unalloyed with base desire and subtle self-love, and takes his stand upon the divine Principles of Purity, Wisdom, Compassion, and Love, incorporating them

into his mind, and manifesting them in his life.
He is now clothed with *the Righteousness of Christ*
(which is incomprehensible to the world) and is rapidly becoming divine. He has not only realized the
darkness of desire; he has also perceived the vanity
of speculative philosophy, and so he rids his mind
of all those metaphysical subtleties which have no
relation to practical holiness, and which have hitherto encumbered his progress, and prevented him
from seeing the enduring realities in life.

And now he casts from him, one after another,
his opinions and speculations, and commences to
live the life of perfect love toward all beings. With
each opinion overcome and abandoned as a burden, there is an increased lightness of spirit, and he
now begins to realize the meaning of being "free."
The divine flowers of Gladness, Joy, and Peace
spring up spontaneously in his heart, and his life
becomes a blissful song. And as the melody in his
heart expands, and grows more and more perfect,
his outward life harmonizes itself with the inward
music. All the effort he puts forth being now free
from strife, he obtains all that is necessary for his
well-being, without pain, anxiety, or fear. He has
almost entirely transcended the competitive laws,
and the Law of Love is now the governing factor
in his life, adjusting all his worldly affairs harmoniously, and without struggle or difficulty on his

part. Indeed, the competitive laws, as they obtain in the commercial world, have here been long left behind, and have ceased to touch him at any point in his material affairs. Here, also, he enters into a wider and more comprehensive consciousness, and, viewing the universe and humanity from the higher altitudes of purity and knowledge to which he has ascended, perceives the orderly sequence of law in all human affairs. The pursuit of this Path brings about the development of still higher powers of mind, arid these powers are—*divine patience, spiritual equanimity, non-resistance,* and *prophetic insight.* By prophetic insight I do not mean the foretelling of events, but direct perception of those hidden causes which operate in human life, and, indeed, in all life, and out of which spring the multifarious and universal effects and events.

The man here rises above the competitive laws as they operate in the thought world, so that their results, which are *violence, ignominy, grief, humiliation,* and *distress* and *anxiety* in all their forms, no more obtain in his life. As he proceeds, the imperishable Principles which form the foundation and fabric of the universe loom before him, and assume more and more symmetrical proportions. For him there is no more anguish; no evil can come near his dwelling; and there breaks upon him the dawning of the abiding Peace.

But he is not yet free. He has not yet finished his journey. He may rest here, and that as long as he chooses; but sooner or later he will rouse himself to the last effort, and will reach the final goal of achievement—the selfless state, the divine life. He is not yet free from self, but still clings, though with less tenacity, to the love of personal existence, and to the idea of exclusive interest in his personal possessions. And when he at last realizes that these selfish elements must also be abandoned, there appears before him the third Gate—*the Gateway of Surrender of Self.* It is no dark portal which he now approaches, but one luminous with divine glory, one radiant with a radiance with which no earthly splendor can vie, and he advances toward it with no uncertain step. The clouds of Doubt have long been dispersed; the sounds of the voices of Temptation are lost in the valley below; and with firm gait, erect carriage, and a heart filled with unspeakable joy, he nears the Gate that guards the Kingdom of God. He has now given up all but self-interest in those things which are his by legal right, but he now perceives that he must hold nothing as his own; and as he pauses at the Gate, he hears the command which cannot be evaded or denied: "Yet lackest thou one thing; sell all that thou hast, and distribute unto the poor, and thou shalt have treasure in Heaven." And passing through the last great

Gate, he stands glorious, radiant, free, detached from the tyranny of desire, of opinion, of self; a divine man—harmless, patient, tender, pure; he has found that for which he has been searching—the Kingdom of God and His Righteousness.

The journey to the Kingdom may be a long and tedious one, or it may be short and rapid. It may occupy a minute, or it may take a thousand ages. Everything depends on the faith and belief of the searcher. The majority cannot "enter in because of their unbelief"; for how can men realize righteousness when they do not believe in it nor in the possibility of its accomplishment? Neither is it necessary to leave the outer world, and one's duties therein. Nay, it can only be found through the unselfish performance of one's duty. Some there are whose faith is so great that, when this truth is presented to them, they can let all the personal elements drop almost immediately out of their minds, and enter into their divine heritage. But all who believe and aspire to achieve will sooner or later arrive at victory if, amid all their worldly duties, they faint not, nor lose sight of the Ideal Goodness, and continue, with unshaken resolve, to "press on to Perfection."

At Rest in the Kingdom and All Things Added

My life is glad–
Nowise forgetting yet those other lives
Painful and poor, wicked and miserable,
Whereon the gods grant pity!

—Sir Edwin Arnold

The whole journey from the Kingdom of Strife to the Kingdom of Love resolves itself into a process which may be summed up in the following words: *The regulation and purification of conduct.* Such a process must, if assiduously pursued, necessarily lead to perfection. It will also be seen that as the man obtains the mastery over certain forces within himself, he arrives at a knowledge of all the laws which operate in the realm of those forces, and by watching the ceaseless working of cause and effect within himself, until he understands it, he then understands it in its universal adjustments in the body of humanity. Moreover, seeing that all the laws which govern human affairs are the direct outcome of the necessities of the human heart, he, having reformed and transmuted those necessities, has brought himself under the guidance of other laws which operate in accordance with his altered condition, and that, having mastered and overcome the selfish forces within himself, he can no longer be subject to the laws which exist for their governance.

The process is also one of *simplification of the mind*, a sifting away of all but the essential gold in character. And as the mind is thus simplified, the apparently unfathomable complexity of the universe assumes simpler and simpler aspects, until the whole is seen to resolve itself into, and to rest upon, a few unalterable Principles; and these Principles are ultimately seen to be contained in *one*, namely LOVE.

The mind thus simplified, the man arrives at peace, and he now really begins to *live*. Looking back on the personal life which he has forever abandoned, he sees it as a horrible nightmare out of which he has awakened; but looking out and down with the eyes of the spirit, he sees that others continue to live it. He sees men and women struggling, fighting, suffering, and perishing for that which is abundantly given to them by the bountiful hand of the Father, if they would only cease from all covetousness, and take it without hurt or hindrance; and compassion fills his heart, and also gladness, for he knows that humanity will wake at last from its long and painful dream. In the early part of his journey he seemed to be leaving humanity far behind, and he sorrowed in his loneliness. But now, having reached the highest, having attained the goal, he finds himself nearer to humanity than ever before—yea, living in its very heart, sympathizing with all its sorrows, rejoicing in all its joys; for, having no longer any personal considerations to defend, he lives entirely in the heart of humanity. He lives no longer for himself; he lives for others; and so living, he enjoys the highest bliss, the deepest peace. For a time he searched for Compassion, Love, Bliss, Truth; but now he has verily become Compassion, Love, Bliss, Truth; and it may literally be said of him that he has ceased to be a personality, for all the personal elements have been extinguished, and there remain only those qualities and principles which are entirely impersonal. And those qualities are now manifested in the man's life, and henceforth *the man's character.*

And having ceased from the protection of self, and living constantly in compassion, wisdom, and

love, he comes under the protection of the highest Law, the Law of Love; and he understands that
Law, and consciously co-operates with it; yea, is
himself inseparately identified with the Law.

Forgoing self, the universe grows I

and he whose nature is compassion, wisdom,
and love cannot possibly need any protection; for
those Principles themselves constitute the highest
protection, being the real, the divine, the immortal in all men, and constituting the indestructible
reality in the cosmic order. Neither does he need
to seek enjoyment whose very nature is Bliss, Joy,
Peace. As for competing with others, with whom
should he compete who has lovingly identified
himself with all? With whom should he struggle
who has sacrificed himself for all? Whose blind,
misguided, and ineffectual competition should he
fear who has reached the source of all blessedness,
and who receives at the hands of the Father all necessary things? Having lost himself (his selfish personality), he has found himself (his divine nature,
Love); and Love and all the effects of Love now
compose his life. He can now joyfully exclaim—

*I have made the acquaintance of the Master of
    Compassion;*

I have put on the Garment of the Perfect Law;
I have entered the realm of the Great Reality;
Wandering is ended, for Rest is accomplished;
Pain and sorrow have ceased, for Peace is entered
    into;
Confusion is dissolved, for Unity is made
    manifest;
Error is vanquished, for Truth is revealed!

The Harmonizing Principle, Righteousness, or Divine Love, being found, all things are seen as they are, and not through the illusory mediums of selfishness and opinion; the universe is *One*, and all its manifold operations are the manifestation of *one Law*. Hitherto in this work *laws* have been referred to, and also spoken of as being *higher* and *lower*, and this distinction was necessary; but now the Kingdom is reached, we see that all the forces operative in human life are the varied manifestations of the One Supreme Law of Love. It is by virtue of this Law that Humanity suffers, that, by the intensity of its sufferings, it shall at last become purified and wise, and so relinquish the source of suffering, which is selfishness.

The Law and foundation of the universe being Love, it follows that all self-seeking is opposed to that Law, is an effort to overcome or ignore the Law, and as a result, every self-seeking act and thought is followed by the exact quota of suffering which is required to annul its effect, and so maintain the universal harmony. All suffering is, therefore, the *restraint* which the Law puts upon ignorance and selfishness, and out of such painful restraint Wisdom at last emerges.

There being no strife and no selfishness in the Kingdom, there is therefore no suffering, no restraint; there is perfect harmony, equipoise, rest. Those who have entered it do not follow any animal inclinations (they have none to follow), but live in accordance with the highest Wisdom. Their nature is Love, and they live in love toward all. They are never troubled about "making a living," as they are Life itself, living in the very Heart of Life; and should any material or other need arise, that need is immediately supplied without any anxiety or struggle on their part. Should they be called to undertake any work, the money and friends needed to carry out that work are immediately forthcoming. Having ceased to violate their principles, all their needs are supplied through legitimate channels. Any money or help required always comes through the instrumentality of good people who are either living in the Kingdom themselves, or are working for its accomplishment.

Those who live in the Kingdom of Love have all their needs supplied by the Law of Love, with all freedom from unrest, just as those who live in the kingdom of self only meet their needs by much strife and suffering. Having altered the root cause in their heart they have altered all the effects in their inner and outer life. As self is the root cause of all strife and suffering, so Love is the root cause of all peace and bliss.

Those who are at rest in the Kingdom do not look for happiness to any outward possession. They see that all such possessions are mere transient effects that come when they are required, and after their purpose is served, pass away. They never think of these things (money, clothing, food, etc.) except as mere accessories and *effects* of the true Life. They are therefore freed from all anxiety and trouble, and resting in Love, they are the embodiment of happiness. Standing upon the imperishable Principles of Purity, Compassion, Wisdom, and Love, they are immortal, and know they are immortal; they are one with God (the Supreme Good), and know they are one with God. Seeing the realities of things, they can find no room anywhere for condemnation. All the operations that obtain upon the earth they see as instruments of the Good Law, even those called *evil*. All men are essentially divine, though unaware of their divine nature, and all their acts are efforts, even though many of them are dark and impotent, to realize some higher good. All so-called evil is seen to be rooted in ignorance, even those deeds that are called *deliberately wicked*, so that condemnation ceases, and Love and Compassion become all in all.

But let it not be supposed that the children of the Kingdom live in ease and indolence (these two sins are the first that have to be eradicated when the search for the Kingdom is entered upon); they live in a peaceful activity; in fact, *they only* truly live, for the life of self with its train of worries, griefs, and fears, is not *real* life. They perform all their duties with the most scrupulous diligence, apart from thoughts of self, and employ all their means, as well as powers and faculties, which are greatly intensified, in building up the Kingdom of Righteousness in the hearts of others and in the world around them. This is their work—first by example, then by precept. Having sold all that they have (renounced all self-interest in their possessions), they now give to the poor (give of their rich store of wisdom, love, and peace to the needy in spirit, the weary and broken-hearted), and follow the Christ whose name is Love. And they sorrow no more, but live in perpetual gladness, for though they see the suffering in the world, they also see the final Bliss and the Eternal Refuge of Love, to which whosoever is ready may come *now*, and to which all will come at last.

The children of the Kingdom *are known by their life*. They manifest the fruits of the Spirit—"love, joy, peace, long-suffering, kindness, goodness, faithfulness, meekness, temperance, self-control"—under all circumstances and vicissitudes. They are entirely free from anger, fear, suspicion, jealousy, caprice, anxiety, and grief. Living in the Righteousness of God, they manifest qualities which are the very reverse of those which obtain in the world, and which are regarded by the world as foolishness. They demand no *rights*; they do not defend themselves; do not retaliate; do good to those who attempt to injure them; manifest the same gentle spirit toward those who oppose and attack them as toward those who agree with them; do not pass judgment on others; condemn no man and no system, and live at peace with all.

The Kingdom of Heaven is perfect trust, perfect knowledge, perfect peace. All is music, sweetness, and tranquillity. No irritations, no bad tempers, no harsh words, no suspicions, no lust, and no disturbing elements can enter there. Its children live in perfect sweetness, forgiving and forgiven, ministering to others with kindly thoughts, words, and deeds. And that Kingdom is in the heart of every man and woman; it is their rightful heritage, their own Kingdom; theirs to enter *now*. But *no sin can enter therein*; no self-born thought or deed can pass its Golden Gates; no impure desire can defile its radiant robes. All may enter it who will, but all *must pay the price*, and that is—*the unconditional abandonment of self.* "If thou wilt be perfect, sell all that thou hast"; but at these words the world turns away "sorrowful, for it is very rich"; rich in money which it cannot keep; rich in fears which it cannot let go; rich in selfish loves to which it greedily clings; rich in grievous partings which it would fain escape; rich in seeking enjoyment; rich in pain and sorrow; rich in strife and suffering; rich in excitement and woe; rich in all things which are not riches, but poor in riches themselves which are not to be found outside the Kingdom; rich in all things that pertain to darkness and death, but poor in those things which are Light and Life.

He, then, who would realize the Kingdom, let him pay the price and enter. If he have a great and holy faith he can do it *now*, and, letting fall from him like a garment the self to which he has been clinging, stand free. If he have less faith, he must rise above self more slowly, and find the Kingdom by daily effort and patient work.

The Temple of Righteousness is built, and its four walls are the four Principles—Purity, Wisdom, Compassion, Love. Peace is its roof, its floor its Steadfastness, its entrance-door is Selfless Duty, its atmosphere is Inspiration, and its music is the Joy of the perfect. It cannot be shaken, and, being eternal and indestructible, there is no more need to seek protection in taking thought for the things of the morrow. And the Kingdom of Heaven being established in the heart, the obtaining of the material necessities of life is no more considered, for, having found the Highest, all these things are added as effect to cause; the struggle for existence has ceased, and the spiritual, mental, and material needs are daily supplied from the universal abundance:

Long I sought thee, Spirit holy,
Master Spirit, meek and lowly;
Sought thee with a silent sorrow, brooding o'er
*   the woes of men;*
Vainly sought thy yoke of meekness
'Neath the weight of woe and weakness;
Finding not, yet in my failing, seeking o'er and
*   o'er again.*

In unrest and doubt and sadness
Dwelt I, yet I knew thy Gladness
Waited somewhere; somewhere greeted torn
*   and sorrowing hearts like mine;*
Knew that somehow I should find thee,
Leaving sin and woe behind me,
And at last thy Love would bid me enter into
*   Rest divine.*

Hatred, mockery, and reviling
Scorched my seeking soul, defiling
That which should have been thy Temple,
wherein thou should'st move and dwell;
Praying, striving, hoping, calling;
Suffering, sorrowing in my falling,
Still I sought thee, groping blindly in the gloomy
depths of Hell.

And I sought thee till I found thee;
And the dark Powers all around me
Fled, and left me silent, peaceful, brooding o'er
thy holy themes;
From within me and without me
Fled they when I ceased to doubt thee;
And I found thee in thy Glory, mighty Master
of my dreams!

Yea, I found thee, Spirit holy,
Beautiful and pure and lowly;
Found thy Joy and Peace and Gladness; found
thee in thy House of Rest;
Found thy strength in Love and Meekness,
And my pain and woe and weakness
Left me, and I walked the Pathway trodden
only by the blest.

Part II
THE HEAVENLY LIFE

The Divine Center

The secret of life, of abundant life, with its strength, its felicity, and its unbroken peace is to find the Divine Center within oneself, and to live in and from that, instead of in that outer circumference of disturbances—the clamors, cravings, and argumentations which make up the animal and intellectual man. These selfish elements constitute the mere husks of life, and must be thrown away by him who would penetrate to the Central Heart of things—to Life itself.

Not to know that within you that is changeless, and defiant of time and death, is not to know anything, but is to play vainly with unsubstantial reflections in the Mirror of Time. Not to find within you those passionless Principles which are not moved by the strifes and shows and vanities of the world is to find nothing but illusions which vanish as they are grasped.

He who resolves that he will not rest satisfied with appearances, shadows, illusions shall, by the piercing light of that resolve, disperse every fleeting phantasy, and shall enter into the substance and reality of life. He shall learn how to live, and he shall live. He shall be the slave of no passion, the servant of no opinion, the votary of no fond error. Finding the Divine Center within his own heart, he will be pure and calm and strong and wise, and will ceaselessly radiate the Heavenly Life in which he lives—*which is himself.*

Having betaken himself to the Divine Refuge within, and remaining there, a man is free from sin. All his yesterdays are as the tide-washed and untrodden sands; no sin shall rise up against him to torment and accuse him and destroy his sacred peace; the fires of remorse cannot scorch him, nor can the storms of regret devastate his dwelling-place. His tomorrows are as seeds which shall germinate, bursting into beauty and potency of life, and no doubt shall shake his trust, no uncertainty rob him of repose. The *Present* is his, only in the immortal Present does he live, and it is as the eternal vault of blue above which looks down silently and calmly, yet radiant with purity and light, upon the upturned and tear-stained faces of the centuries.

Men love their desires, for gratification seems sweet to them, but its end is pain and vacuity; they love the argumentations of the intellect, for egotism seems most desirable to them, but the fruits thereof are humiliation and sorrow. When the soul has reached the end of gratification and reaped the bitter fruits of egotism, it is ready to receive the Divine Wisdom and to enter into the Divine Life. Only the crucified can be transfigured; only by the death of self can the Lord of the heart rise again into the Immortal Life, and stand radiant upon the Olivet of Wisdom.

Thou hast thy trials? Every outward trial is the replica of an inward imperfection. Thou shalt grow wise by knowing this, and shalt thereby transmute trial into active joy, finding the Kingdom where trial cannot come. When wilt thou learn thy lessons, O child of earth! All thy sorrows cry out against thee; every pain is thy just accuser, and thy griefs are but the shadows of thy unworthy and perishable self. The Kingdom of Heaven is thine; how long wilt thou reject it, preferring the lurid atmosphere of Hell—the hell of thy self-seeking self?

Where self is not, there is the Garden of the Heavenly Life, and

> *There spring the healing streams*
>> *Quenching all thirst! there bloom the*
>> *immortal flowers*
> *Carpeting all the way with joy! there throng*
>> *Swiftest and sweetest hours!*

The redeemed sons of God, the glorified in body and spirit, are "bought with a price," and that price is the crucifixion of the personality, the death of self; and having put away that within which is the source of all discord, they have found the universal Music, the abiding Joy.

Life is more than motion, it is Music; more than rest, it is Peace; more than work, it is Duty; more than labor, it is Love; more than enjoyment, it is Blessedness; more than acquiring money and position and reputation, it is Knowledge, Purpose, strong and high Resolve.

Let the impure turn to Purity, and they shall be pure; let the weak resort to Strength, and they shall be strong; let the ignorant fly to Knowledge, and they shall be wise. All things are man's, and he chooses that which he will have. Today he chooses in ignorance, tomorrow he shall choose in Wisdom. He shall "work out his own salvation" whether he believe it or not, for he cannot escape himself, nor transfer to another the eternal responsibility of his own soul. By no theological subterfuge shall he trick the Law of his being, which shall shatter all his selfish makeshifts and excuses for right thinking and right doing. Nor shall God do for him that which it is destined his soul shall accomplish for itself. What would you say of a man who, wanting to possess a mansion in which to dwell peacefully, purchased the site and then knelt down and asked God to build the house for him? Would you not say that such a man was foolish? And of another man who, having purchased the land, set the architects and builders and carpenters at work to erect the edifice, would you not say that he was wise? And as it is in the building of a material house, even so it is in the building of a spiritual mansion. Brick by brick, pure thought upon pure thought, good deed upon good deed, must the habitation of a blameless life rise from its sure foundation until at last it stands out in all the majesty of its faultless proportions. Not by caprice, nor gift, nor favor does a man obtain the spiritual realities, but by diligence, watchfulness, energy, and effort.

Strong is the soul, and wise and beautiful;
The seeds of God-like power are in us still;
Gods are we, bards, saints, heroes, if we will.

The spiritual Heart of man is the Heart of the universe, and, finding that Heart, man finds the strength to accomplish all things. He finds there also the Wisdom to see things as they are. He finds there the Peace that is divine. At the center of man's being is the Music which orders the stars— the Eternal Harmony. He who would find Blessedness, let him find himself; let him abandon every discordant desire, every inharmonious thought, every unlovely habit and deed, and he will find that Grace and Beauty and Harmony which form the indestructible essence of his own being.

Men fly from creed to creed, and find— unrest; they travel in many lands, and discover— disappointment; they build themselves beautiful mansions, and plant pleasant gardens, and reap— ennui and discomfort. Not until a man falls back upon the Truth within himself does he find rest and satisfaction; not until he builds the inward Mansion of Faultless Conduct does he find the endless and incorruptible Joy, and, having obtained that, he will infuse it into all his outward doings and possessions.

If a man would have peace, let him exercise the spirit of Peace; if he would find love, let him dwell in the spirit of Love; if he would escape suffering, let him cease to inflict it; if he would do noble things for humanity, let him cease to do ignoble things for himself. If he will but quarry the mine of his own soul, he shall find there all the materials for building whatsoever he will, and he shall find there also the central Rock on which to build in safety.

Howsoever a man works to right the world, it will never be righted until he has put himself right. This may be written upon the heart as a mathematical axiom. It is not enough to preach Purity, men must cease from lust; to exhort to love, they must abandon hatred; to extol self-sacrifice, they must yield up self; to adorn with mere words the Perfect Life, they must *be* perfect.

When a man can no longer carry the weight of his many sins, let him fly to the Christ, whose throne is the center of his own heart, and he shall become lighthearted, entering the glad company of the Immortals.

When he can no longer bear the burden of his accumulated learning, let a man leave his books, his science, his philosophy, and come back to himself, and he shall find within that which he outwardly sought and found not—his own divinity.

He ceases to argue about God who has found God within. Relying upon that calm strength which is not the strength of self, he *lives* God, manifesting in his daily life the Highest Goodness, which is Eternal Life.

The Eternal Now

Now is the reality in which time is contained. It is more and greater than time; it is an ever-present reality. It knows neither past nor future, and is eternally potent and substantial. Every minute, every day, every year is a dream as soon as it has passed, and exists only as an imperfect and unsubstantial picture in the memory, if it be not entirely obliterated.

Past and future are dreams; *now* is a reality. All things are now; all power, all possibility, all action is now. Not to act and accomplish now is not to act and accomplish at all. To live in thoughts of what you might have done, or in dreams of what you mean to do, this is folly; but to put away regret, to anchor anticipation, and to do and to work *now*, this is wisdom.

While a man is dwelling upon the past or future he is missing the present; he is forgetting to live now. All things are possible now, and *only* now. Without wisdom to guide him, and mistaking the unreal for the real, a man says, "If I had done so and so last week, last month, or last year, it would have been better with me today"; or, "I know what is best to be done, and I will do it tomorrow." The selfish cannot comprehend the vast importance and value of the present, and fail to see it as the substantial reality of which past and future are the empty reflections. It may truly be said that past and future do not exist except as negative shadows, and to live in them— that is, in the regretful and selfish contemplation of them—is to miss the reality in life.

The Present, the Present is all thou hast
*   For thy sure possessing;*
Like the patriarch's angel, hold it fast,
*   Till it gives its blessing.*

All which is real now remaineth,
*   And fadeth never:*
The hand which upholds it now sustaineth
*   The soul for ever.*

Then of what is to be, and of what is done,
*   Why queriest thou?*

The past and the time to be are one,
*   And both are NOW!*

Man has all power now; but not knowing this, he says, "I will be perfect next year, or in so many years, or in so many lives." The dwellers in the Kingdom of God, who live only in the now, say, "I am perfect now," and refraining from all sin now, and cease-lessly guarding the portals of the mind, not looking to the past nor to the future, nor turning to the left or right, they remain eternally holy and blessed. "Now is the accepted time; now is the day of salvation."

Say to yourself, "I will live in my Ideal now; I will manifest my Ideal now; I will be my Ideal now; and all that tempts me away from my Ideal I will not listen to; I will listen only to the voice of my Ideal." Thus resolving and thus doing, you shall not depart from the Highest, and shall eternally manifest the True.

Afoot and light-hearted, I take to the open road.
Henceforth I ask not good fortune: I myself am
*   good fortune.*
Henceforth I whimper no more, postpone no
*   more, need nothing;*
Done with indoor complaints, libraries,
*   querulous criticisms.*
Strong and content, I take to the open road.

Cease to tread every byway of dependence, every winding side-way that tempts thy soul into the shadow-land of the past and the future, and manifest thy native and divine strength now. Come out into "the open road."

That which you would be, and hope to be, you may be now. Non-accomplishment resides in your perpetual postponement, and, having the power to postpone, you also have the power to accomplish— to perpetually accomplish: realize this truth, and you shall be today, and every day, the ideal man of whom you dreamed.

Virtue consists in fighting sin day after day, but holiness consists in leaving sin, unnoticed and ignored, to die by the wayside; and this is done, can only be done, in the living now. Say not unto thy soul, "Thou shalt be purer tomorrow"; but rather say, "Thou shalt be pure now." Tomorrow is too late for anything, and he who sees his help and salvation in to-morrow shall continually fail and fall Today.

Thus didst fall yesterday? Didst sin grievously? Having realized this, leave it instantly and forever, and watch that thou sinnest not now. The while thou art bewailing the past every gate of thy soul remains unguarded against the entrance of sin now. Thou shall not rise by grieving over the irre-mediable past, but by remedying the present.

The foolish man, loving the boggy side-path of procrastination rather than the firm Highway of Present Effort, says, "I will rise early tomorrow; I will get out of debt tomorrow; I will carry out my intentions tomorrow." But the wise man, realizing the momentous import of the Eternal Now, rises early today; keeps out of debt today; carries out his intentions today; and so never departs from strength and peace and ripe accomplishment.

That which is done now remains; that which is to be done tomorrow does not appear. It is wisdom to leave that which has not arrived, and to attend to that which is; and to attend to it with such a consecration of soul and concentration of effort as shall leave no possible loophole for regret to creep in.

A man's spiritual comprehension being clouded by the illusions of self, he says, "I was born on such a day, so many years ago, and shall die at my allotted time." But he was not born, neither will he die, for how can that which is immortal, which eternally *is*, be subject to birth and death? Let a man throw off his illusions, and then he will see that the birth and death of the *body* are the mere incidents of a journey, and not its beginning and end.

Looking back to happy beginnings, and forward to mournful endings, a man's eyes are blinded, so that he beholds not his own immortality; his ears are closed, so that he hears not the ever-present harmonies of Joy; and his heart is hardened, so that it pulsates not to the rhythmic sounds of Peace.

The universe, with all that it contains, is now. Put out thy hand, O man, and receive the fruits of Wisdom! Cease from thy greedy striving, thy selfish sorrowing, thy foolish regretting, and be content to *live*. Act now, and, lo! all things are done; live now, and, behold! thou art in the midst of Plenty; *be* now, and *know* that thou art perfect.

The "Original Simplicity"

L ife is simple. Being is simple. The universe is simple. Complexity arises in ignorance and self-delusion. The "Original Simplicity" of Lao-tze is a term expressive of the universe as it *is*, and not as it *appears*. Looking through the woven network of his own illusions, man sees interminable complication and unfathomable mystery, and so loses himself in the labyrinths of his own making. Let a man put away egotism, and he will see the universe in all the beauty of its pristine simplicity. Let him annihilate the delusion of the personal "I," and he will destroy all the illusions which spring from that "I." He will thus "re-become a little child," and will "revert to Original Simplicity."

When a man succeeds in entirely forgetting (annihilating) his personal self, he becomes a mirror in which the universal Reality is faultlessly reflected. He is awakened, and henceforward he lives, not in dreams, but realities.

Pythagoras saw the universe in the ten numbers, but even this simplicity may be further reduced, and the universe ultimately be found to be contained in the number ONE, for all the numerals and all their Infinite complications are but additions of the *One*.

Let life cease to be lived as a fragmentary thing, and let it be lived as a perfect Whole; the simplicity of the Perfect will then be revealed. How shall the fragment comprehend the Whole? Yet how simple that the Whole should comprehend the fragment. How shall sin perceive Holiness? Yet how plain that Holiness should understand sin. He who would become the Greater let him abandon the lesser. In no form is the circle contained, but in the circle all forms are contained. In no color is the radiant light imprisoned, but in the radiant light all colors are embodied. Let a man destroy all the forms of self, and he shall apprehend the Circle of Perfection; let him submerge, in the silent depths of his being, the varying colors of his thoughts and desires, and he shall be illuminated with the White Light of Divine Knowledge. In the perfect chord of music the single note, though forgotten, is indispensably contained, and the drop of water becomes of supreme usefulness by losing itself in the ocean. Sink thyself compassionately in the heart of humanity, and thou shalt reproduce the harmonies of Heaven; lose thyself in unlimited love toward all, and thou shalt work enduring works and shalt become one with the eternal Ocean of Bliss.

Man evolves outward to the periphery of complexity, and then involves backward to the Central Simplicity. When a man discovers that it is mathematically impossible for him to know the universe before knowing himself, he then starts upon the Way which leads to the Original Simplicity. He begins to unfold from within, and as he unfolds himself, he enfolds the universe.

Cease to speculate about God, and find the all-embracing Good within thee, then shalt thou see the emptiness and vanity of speculation, knowing thyself one with God.

He who will not give up his secret lust, his covetousness, his anger, his opinion about this or that can see nor know nothing; he will remain a dullard in the school of Wisdom, though he be accounted learned in the colleges.

If a man would find the Key of Knowledge, let him find himself. Thy sins are not thyself; they are not any part of thyself; they are diseases which thou hast come to love. Cease to cling to them, and they will no longer cling to thee. Let them fall away, and thy self shall stand revealed. Thou shalt then know thyself as Comprehensive Vision, Invincible Principle, Immortal Life, and eternal Good.

The impure man believes impurity to be his rightful condition, but the pure man knows himself as pure being; he also, penetrating the Veils, sees all others as pure being. Purity is extremely simple, and needs no argument to support it; impurity is interminably complex, and is ever involved in defensive argument. Truth *lives* itself. A blameless life is the only witness of Truth. Men cannot see, and will not accept the witness until they find it within themselves; and having found it, a man becomes silent before his fellows. Truth is so simple that it cannot be found in the region of argument and advertisement, and so silent that it is only manifested in actions.

So extremely simple is Original Simplicity that a man must let go his hold of everything before he can perceive it. The great arch is strong by virtue of the hollowness underneath, and a wise man becomes strong and invincible by emptying himself.

Meekness, Patience, Love, Compassion, and Wisdom—these are the dominant qualities of Original Simplicity; therefore the imperfect cannot understand it. Wisdom only can apprehend Wisdom; therefore the fool says, "No man is wise." The imperfect man says, "No man can be perfect," and he therefore remains where he is. Though he live with a perfect man all his life, he shall not behold his perfection. Meekness he will call cowardice; Patience, Love, and Compassion he will see as weakness; and Wisdom will appear to him as folly. Faultless discrimination belongs to the Perfect Whole, and resides not in any part; therefore men are exhorted to refrain from judgment until they have themselves manifested the Perfect Life.

Arriving at Original Simplicity, opacity disappears, and the universal transparency becomes apparent. He who has found the indwelling Reality of his own being has found the original and universal Reality. Knowing the Divine Heart within, all hearts are known, and the thoughts of all men become his who has become the master of his own thoughts; therefore the good man does not defend himself, but molds the minds of others to his own likeness.

As the problematical transcends crudity, so Pure Goodness transcends the problematical. All problems vanish when Pure Goodness is reached; therefore the good man is called "The slayer of illusions." What problem can vex where sin is not? O thou who strivest loudly and restest not! Retire

into the holy silence of thine own being, and live
therefrom. So shalt thou, finding Pure Goodness,
rend in twain the Veil of the Temple of Illusion,
and shalt enter into the Patience, Peace, and tran-
scendent Glory of the Perfect, for Pure Goodness
and Original Simplicity are one.

The
Unfailing Wisdom

A man should be superior to his possessions, his body, his circumstances and surroundings, and the opinions of others and their attitude toward him. Until he is this, he is not strong and steadfast. He should also rise superior to his own desires and opinions; and until he is this, he is not wise.

The man who identifies himself with his possessions will feel that all is lost when these are lost; he who regards himself as the outcome and the tool of circumstances will weakly fluctuate with every change in his outward condition; and great will be his unrest and pain who seeks to stand upon the approbation of others.

To detach oneself from every outward thing, and to rest securely upon the inward Virtue, this is the Unfailing Wisdom. Having this Wisdom, a man will be the same whether in riches or poverty. The one cannot add to his strength, nor the other rob him of his serenity. Neither can riches defile him who has washed away all the inward defilement, nor the lack of them degrade him who has ceased to degrade the temple of his soul.

To refuse to be enslaved by any outward thing or happening, regarding all such things and happenings as for your use, for your education, this is Wisdom. To the wise all occurrences are *good*, and, having no eye for evil, they grow wiser every day. They utilize all things, and thus put all things under their feet. They see all their mistakes as soon as made, and accept them as lessons of intrinsic value, knowing that there are no mistakes in the Divine Order. They thus rapidly approach the Divine Perfection. They are moved by none, yet learn from all. They crave love from none, yet give love to all. To learn, and not to be shaken; to love where one is not loved; herein lies the strength which shall never fail a man. The man who says in his heart, "I will teach all men, and learn from none" will neither teach nor learn while he is in that frame of mind, but will remain in his folly.

All strength and wisdom and power and knowledge a man will find within himself, but he will not find it in egotism; he will only find it in obedience, submission, and willingness to learn. He must obey the Higher, and not glorify himself in the lower. He who stands upon egotism, rejecting reproof, instruction, and the lessons of experience, will surely fall; yea, he is already fallen. Said a great Teacher to his disciples, "Those who shall be a lamp unto themselves, relying upon themselves only, and not relying upon any external help, but holding fast to the Truth as their lamp, and, seeking their salvation in the Truth alone, shall not look for assistance to any besides themselves, it is they among my disciples who shall reach the very topmost height! *But they must be willing to learn.*" The wise man is always anxious to learn, but never anxious to teach, for he knows that the true Teacher is in the heart of every man, and must ultimately be found there by all. The foolish man, being governed largely by vanity, is very anxious to teach, but unwilling to learn, not having found the Holy Teacher within who speaks wisdom to the humbly listening soul. Be self-reliant, but let thy self-reliance be saintly and not selfish.

Folly and wisdom, weakness and strength are within a man, and not in any external thing, neither do they spring from any external cause. A man cannot be strong for another, he can only be strong for himself; he cannot overcome for another, he can only overcome of himself. You may learn of another, but you must accomplish for yourself. Put away all external props, and rely upon the Truth within you. A creed will not bear a man up in the hour of temptation; he must possess the inward Knowledge which slays temptation. A speculative philosophy will prove a shadowy thing in the time of calamity; a man must have the inward Wisdom which puts an end to grief.

Goodness, which is the aim of all religions, is distinct from religions themselves. Wisdom, which is the aim of every philosophy, is distinct from all philosophies. The Unfailing Wisdom is found only by constant practice in pure thinking and well-doing, by harmonizing one's mind and heart to those things which are beautiful, lovable, and true.

In whatever condition a man finds himself, he can always find the True; and he can find it only by so utilizing his present condition as to become strong and wise. The effeminate hankering after rewards, and the craven fear of punishment, let them be put away forever, and let a man joyfully bend himself to the faithful performance of all his duties, forgetting himself and his worthless pleasures, and living strong and pure and self-contained; so shall he surely find the Unfailing Wisdom, the God-like Patience and strength. "The situation that has not its Duty, its Ideal, was never yet occupied by man. . . . Here or nowhere is thy

Ideal. Work it out therefrom, and, working, believe, live, be free. The Ideal is in thyself, the impediment, too, is in thyself; thy condition is but the stuff thou art to shape that same Ideal out of. What matters whether such stuff be of this sort or that, so the form thou give it be heroic, be poetic? Oh, thou that pinest in the imprisonment of the Actual, and criest bitterly to the gods for a kingdom wherein to rule and create, know this of a truth: the thing thou seekest is already within thee, here and now, couldest thou only see!"

All that is beautiful and blessed is in thyself, not in thy neighbor's wealth. Thou art poor? Thou art poor indeed if thou art not stronger than thy poverty! Thou hast suffered calamities? Well, wilt thou cure calamity by adding anxiety to it? Canst thou mend a broken vase by weeping over it, or restore a lost delight by thy lamentations? There is no evil but will vanish if thou wilt wisely meet it. The God-like soul does not grieve over that which has been, is, or will be, but perpetually finds the Divine Good, and gains wisdom by every occurrence.

Fear is the shadow of selfishness, and cannot live where loving Wisdom is. Doubt, anxiety, and worry are unsubstantial shades in the underworld of self, and shall no more trouble him who will climb the serene altitudes of his soul. Grief, also, will be forever dispelled by him who will comprehend the Law of his being. He who so comprehends shall find the Supreme Law of Life, and he shall find that it is Love, that it is imperishable Love. He shall become one with that Love, and loving all, with mind freed from all hatred and folly, he shall receive the invincible protection which Love affords. Claiming nothing, he shall suffer no loss; seeking no pleasure, he shall find no grief; and employing all his powers as instruments of service, he shall evermore live in the highest state of blessedness and bliss.

Know this: Thou makest and unmakest thyself; thou standest and fallest by what thou art. Thou art a slave if thou preferrest to be; thou art a master if thou wilt make thyself one. Build upon thy animal desires and intellectual opinions, and thou buildest upon the sand; build upon Virtue and Holiness, and no wind nor tide shall shake thy strong abode. So shall the Unfailing Wisdom uphold thee in every emergency, and the Everlasting Arms gather thee to thy peace.

Lay up each year
Thy harvest of well-doing, wealth that kings
Nor thieves can take away. When all the things
Thou callest thine, goods, pleasures, honors fall,
Thou in thy virtue shalt survive them all.

The Might
of Meekness

The mountain bends not to the fiercest storm, but it shields the fledgling and the lamb; and though all men tread upon it, yet it protects them, and bears them up upon its deathless bosom. Even so is it with the meek man who, though shaken and disturbed by none, yet compassionately bends to shield the lowliest creature, and, though he may be despised, lifts all men up, and lovingly protects them.

As glorious as the mountain in its silent might is the divine man in his silent Meekness; like its form, his loving compassion is expansive and sublime. Truly his body, like the mountain's base, is fixed in the valleys and the mists; but the summit of his being is eternally bathed in cloudless glory, and lives with the Silences.

He who has found Meekness has found divinity; he has realized the divine consciousness, and knows himself as divine. He also knows all others as divine, though they know it not themselves, being asleep and dreaming. Meekness is a divine quality, and as such is all-powerful. The meek man overcomes by not resisting, and by allowing himself to be defeated he attains to the Supreme Conquest.

The man who conquers another by force is strong; the man who conquers himself by Meekness is mighty. He who conquers another by force will himself likewise be conquered; he who conquers himself by Meekness will never be overthrown, for the human cannot overcome the divine. The meek man is triumphant in defeat. Socrates lives the more by being put to death; in the crucified Jesus the risen Christ is revealed, and Stephen in receiving his stoning defies the hurting power of stones. That which is real cannot be destroyed, but only that which is unreal. When a man finds that within him which is real, which is constant, abiding, changeless, and eternal, he enters into that Reality, and becomes meek. All the powers of darkness will come against him, but they will do him no hurt, and will at last depart from him.

The meek man is found in the time of trial; when other men fall he stands. His patience is not destroyed by the foolish passions of others, and when they come against him he does not "strive nor cry." He knows the utter powerlessness of all evil, having overcome it in himself, and lives in the changeless strength and power of divine Good.

Meekness is one aspect of the operation of that changeless Love which is at the Heart of all things, and is therefore an imperishable quality. He who lives in it is without fear, knowing the Highest, and having the lowest under his feet.

The meek man shines in darkness, and flourishes in obscurity. Meekness cannot boast, nor advertise itself, nor thrive on popularity. It is *practiced*, and is seen or not seen; being a spiritual quality it is perceived only by the eye of the spirit. Those who are not spiritually awakened see it not, nor do they love it, being enamored of, and blinded by, worldly shows and appearances. Nor does history take note of the meek man. Its glory is that of strife and self-aggrandizement; his is the glory of peace and gentleness. History chronicles the earthly, not the heavenly acts. Yet though he lives in obscurity he cannot be hidden (how can light be hid?); he continues to shine after he has withdrawn himself from the world, and is worshiped by the world which knew him not.

That the meek man should be neglected, abused, or misunderstood is reckoned by him as of no account, and therefore not to be considered, much less resisted. He knows that all such weapons are the flimsiest and most ineffectual of shadows. To them, therefore, who give him evil he gives good. He resists none, and thereby conquers all.

He who imagines he can be injured by others, and who seeks to justify and defend himself against them, does not understand Meekness, does not comprehend the essence and meaning of life. "He abused me, he beat me, he defeated me, he robbed me. In those who harbor such thoughts hatred will never cease . . . for hatred ceases not by hatred at any time; hatred ceases by love." What sayest thou, thy neighbor has spoken of thee falsely? Well, what of that? Can a falsity hurt thee? That which is false is false, and there is an end of it. It is without life, and without power to hurt any but him who seeks to hurt by it. It is nothing to thee that thy neighbor should speak falsely of thee, but it is much to thee that thou shouldst resist him, and seek to justify thyself, for, by so doing, thou givest life and vitality to thy neighbor's falseness, so that thou art injured and distressed. Take all evil out of thine own heart, then shalt thou see the folly of resisting it in another. Thou wilt be trodden on? Thou art trodden on already if thou thinkest thus. The injury that thou seest as coming from another comes only from thyself. The wrong thought, or word, or act of another has no power to hurt thee unless thou galvanize it into life by thy passionate resistance, and so receivest it into thyself. If any man slander me, that is his concern, not mine. I have to do with my own soul, not with my neighbor's. Though all the world misjudge me, it is no business of mine; but that I should possess my soul in Purity and Love, that is all my business. There shall be no end to strife until men cease to justify themselves. He who would have wars cease let him cease to defend any party—let him cease to defend himself. Not by strife can peace come, but by ceasing from strife. The glory of Caesar resides in the resistance of his enemies. They resist and fall. Give to Caesar that which Caesar demands, and Caesar's glory and power are gone. Thus, by submission does the meek man conquer the strong man; but it is not that outward show of submission which is slavery, it is that inward and spiritual submission which is *freedom*.

Claiming no *rights*, the meek man is not troubled with self-defense and self-justification; he lives in love, and therefore comes under the immediate and vital protection of the Great Love which is the Eternal Law of the universe. He neither claims nor seeks his own; thus do all things come to him, and all the universe shields and protects him.

He who says, "I have tried Meekness, and it has failed" has not tried Meekness. It cannot be tried as an experiment. It is only arrived at by unreserved self-sacrifice. Meekness does not consist merely in non-resistance in action; it consists preeminently in non-resistance in *thought*, in ceasing to hold or to have any selfish, condemnatory, or retaliatory thoughts. The meek man, therefore, cannot "take offense" or have his "feelings hurt," living above hatred, folly, and vanity. Meekness can never fail.

O thou who searchest for the Heavenly Life! Strive after Meekness; increase thy patience and forbearance day by day; bid thy tongue cease from all harsh words; withdraw thy mind from selfish arguments, and refuse to brood upon thy wrongs; so living, thou shalt carefully tend and cultivate the pure and delicate flower of Meekness in thy heart, until at last, its divine sweetness and purity and beauteous perfection shall be revealed to thee, and thou shalt become gentle, joyful, and strong. Repine not that thou art surrounded by irritable and selfish people; but rather rejoice that thou art so favored as to have thine own imperfections revealed to thee, and that thou art so placed as to necessitate within thee a constant struggle for self-mastery and the attainment of perfection. The more there is of harshness and selfishness around thee, the greater is the need of thy Meekness and love. If others seek to wrong thee, all the more is it needful that thou shouldst cease from all wrong, and live in love; if others preach Meekness, humility, and love, and do not practice these, trouble not, nor be annoyed; but do thou, in the silence of thy heart, and in thy contact with others, *practice* these things, and they shall preach themselves. And though thou utter no declamatory word, and stand before no gathered audience, thou shalt teach the whole world. As thou becomest meek, thou shalt learn the deepest secrets of the universe. Nothing is hidden from him who overcomes himself. Into the cause of causes shalt thou penetrate, and lifting, one after another, every veil of illusion, shalt reach at last the inmost Heart of Being. Thus becoming one with Life, thou shalt know all life, and, seeing into causes, and knowing realities, thou shalt be no more anxious about thyself, and others, and the world, but shalt see that all things that are are engines of the Great Law. Canopied with gentleness, thou shalt bless where others curse; love where others hate; forgive where others condemn; yield where others strive; give up where others grasp; lose where others gain. And in their strength they shall be weak; and in thy weakness thou shalt be strong; yea, thou shalt mightily prevail. He that hath not unbroken gentleness hath not Truth:

> *Therefore when Heaven would save a man, it enfolds him with gentleness.*

The
Righteous Man

The righteous man is invincible. No enemy can possibly overcome or confound him; and he needs no other protection than that of his own integrity and holiness.

As it is impossible for evil to overcome Good, so the righteous man can never be brought low by the unrighteous. Slander, envy, hatred, malice can never reach him, nor cause him any suffering, and those who try to injure him only succeed ultimately in bringing ignominy upon themselves.

The righteous man, having nothing to hide, committing no acts which require stealth, and harboring no thoughts and desires which he would not like others to know, is fearless and unashamed. His step is firm, his body upright, and his speech direct and without ambiguity. He looks everybody in the face. How can he fear any who wrongs none? How can he be ashamed before any who deceives none? And ceasing from all wrong he can never be wronged; ceasing from all deceit he can never be deceived.

The righteous man, performing all his duties with scrupulous diligence, and living above sin, is invulnerable at every point. He who has slain the inward enemies of virtue can never be brought low by any outward enemy; neither does he need to seek any protection against them, righteousness being an all-sufficient protection.

The unrighteous man is vulnerable at almost every point; living in his passions, the slave of prejudices, impulses, and ill-formed opinions, he is continually suffering (as he imagines) at the hands of others. The slanders, attacks, and accusations of others cause him great suffering because they have a basis of truth in himself; and not having the protection of righteousness, he endeavors to justify and protect himself by resorting to retaliation and specious argument, and even to subterfuge and deceit.

The partially righteous man is vulnerable at all those points where he falls short of righteousness, and should the righteous man fall from his righteousness, and give way to *one* sin, his invincibility is gone, for he has thereby placed himself where attack and accusation can justly reach and injure him, because he has first injured himself.

If a man suffers or is injured through the instrumentality of others, let him look to himself, and, putting aside self-pity and self-defense, he will find in his own heart the source of all his woe.

No evil can happen to the righteous man who has cut off the source of evil in himself; living in the All-Good, and abstaining from sin in thought, word, and deed, whatever happens to him is good; neither can any person, event, or circumstance cause him suffering, for the tyranny of circumstance is utterly destroyed for him who has broken the bonds of sin.

The suffering, the sorrowing, the weary, and broken-hearted ever seek a sorrowless refuge, a haven of perpetual peace. Let such fly to the refuge of the righteous life; let them come now and enter the haven of the sinless state, for sorrow cannot overtake the righteous; suffering cannot reach him who does not waste in self-seeking his spiritual substance; and he cannot be afflicted by weariness and unrest whose heart is at peace with all.

Perfect Love

The Children of Light, who abide in the Kingdom of Heaven, see the universe, and all that it contains, as the manifestation of one Law—the Law of Love. They see Love as the molding, sustaining, protecting, and perfecting Power immanent in all things animate and inanimate. To them Love is not merely and only a rule of life, it is the Law of Life, it is Life itself. Knowing this, they order their whole life in accordance with Love, not regarding their own personality. By thus practicing obedience to the Highest, to divine Love, they become conscious partakers of the power of Love, and so arrive at perfect Freedom as Masters of Destiny.

The universe is preserved because Love is at the Heart of it. Love is the only preservative power.

While there is hatred in the heart of man, he imagines the Law to be cruel, but when his heart is mellowed by Compassion and Love, he perceives that the Law is Infinite Kindness. So kind is the Law that it protects man against his own ignorance. Man, in his puny efforts to subvert the Law by attaching undue importance to his own little personality, brings upon himself such trains of suffering that he is at last compelled, in the depth of his afflictions, to seek for Wisdom; and finding Wisdom, he finds Love, and knows it as the Law of his being, the Law of the universe. Love does not punish; man punishes himself by his own hatred; by striving to preserve evil which has no life by which to preserve itself, and by trying to subvert Love, which can neither be overcome nor destroyed, being of the substance of Life. When a man burns himself, does he accuse the fire? Therefore, when a man suffers, let him look for some ignorance or disobedience within himself.

Love is Perfect Harmony, pure Bliss, and contains, therefore, no element of suffering. Let a man think no thought and do no act which is not in accordance with pure Love, and suffering shall no more trouble him. If a man would know Love, and partake of its undying bliss, he must practice it in his heart; he must become Love.

He who always acts from the spirit of Love is never deserted, is never left in a dilemma or difficulty, for Love (impersonal Love) is both Knowledge and Power. He who has learned how to Love has learned how to master every difficulty, how to transmute every failure into success, how to clothe every event and condition in garments of blessedness and beauty.

The way to Love is by self-mastery, and, traveling that way, a man builds himself up in Knowledge as he proceeds. Arriving at Love, he enters into full possession of body and mind, by right of the divine Power which he has earned.

"Perfect Love casteth out fear." To know Love is to know that there is no harmful power in the whole universe. Even sin itself, which the worldly and unbelieving imagine is so unconquerable, is known as a very weak and perishable thing that shrinks away and disappears before the compelling power of Good. Perfect Love is perfect Harmlessness. And he who has destroyed, in himself, all thoughts of harm, and all desire to harm, receives the universal protection, and knows himself to be invincible.

Perfect Love is perfect Patience. Anger and irritability cannot dwell with it nor come near it. It sweetens every bitter occasion with the perfume of holiness, and transmutes trial into divine strength. Complaint is foreign to it. He who loves bewails nothing, but accepts all things and conditions as heavenly guests; he is therefore constantly blessed, and sorrow does not overtake him.

Perfect Love is perfect Trust. He who has destroyed the desire to grasp can never be troubled with the fear of loss. Loss and gain are alike foreign to him. Steadfastly maintaining a loving attitude of mind toward all, and pursuing, in the performance of his duties, a constant and loving activity, Love protects him and evermore supplies him in fullest measure with all that he needs.

Perfect Love is perfect Power. The wisely loving heart commands without exercising any authority. All things and all men obey him who obeys the Highest. He thinks, and lo! he has already accomplished! He speaks, and behold! a world hangs upon his simple utterances! He has harmonized his thoughts with the Imperishable and Unconquerable Forces, and for him weakness and uncertainty are no more. His every thought is a purpose; his every act an accomplishment; he moves with the Great Law, not setting his puny personal will against it, and he thus becomes a channel through which the divine Power can flow in unimpeded and beneficent expression. He has thus become Power itself.

Perfect Love is perfect Wisdom. The man who loves all is the man who knows all. Having thoroughly learned the lessons of his own heart, he knows the tasks and trials of other hearts, and adapts himself to them gently and without ostentation. Love illuminates the intellect; without it the intellect is blind and cold and lifeless. Love succeeds where the intellect fails; sees where the intellect is blind; knows where the intellect is ignorant. Reason is only completed in Love, and is ultimately absorbed in it. Love is the Supreme Reality in the universe, and as such it contains all Truth. Infinite Tenderness enfolds and cherishes the universe; therefore is the wise man gentle and childlike and tender-hearted. He sees that the one thing which all creatures need is Love, and he gives unstintingly. He knows that all occasions require the adjusting power of Love, and he ceases from harshness.

To the eye of Love all things are revealed, not as an infinity of complex effects, but in the light of Eternal Principles, out of which spring all causes and effects, and back into which they return. "God is Love"; therefore than Love there is nothing more perfect. He who would find pure knowledge, let him find pure Love.

Perfect Love is perfect Peace. He who dwells with it has completed his pilgrimage in the underworld of sorrow. With mind calm and heart at rest, he has banished the shadows of grief, and knows the deathless Life.

If thou wouldst perfect thyself in Knowledge, perfect thyself in Love. If thou wouldst reach the Highest, ceaselessly cultivate a loving and compassionate heart.

Perfect Freedom

There is no bondage in the Heavenly Life. There is Perfect Freedom. This is its great glory. This Supreme Freedom is gained only by obedience. He who obeys the Highest cooperates with the Highest, and so masters every force within himself and every condition without. A man may choose the lower and neglect the Higher, but the Higher is never overcome by the lower; herein lies the revelation of Freedom. Let a man choose the Higher and abandon the lower; he shall then establish himself as an Overcomer, and shall realize Perfect Freedom.

To give the reins to inclination is the only slavery; to conquer oneself is the only freedom. The slave to self loves his chains, and will not have one of them broken for fear he would be depriving himself of some cherished delight. He clings to his gratifications and vanities, regarding freedom from them as an empty and undesirable condition. He thus defeats and enslaves himself.

By self-enlightenment is Perfect Freedom found. While a man remains ignorant of himself, of his desires, of his emotions and thoughts, and of the inward causes which mold his life and destiny, having neither control nor understanding of himself, he will remain in bondage to passion, sorrow, suffering, and fluctuating fortune. The Land of Perfect Freedom lies through the Gate of Knowledge.

All outward oppression is but the shadow and effect of the real oppression within. For ages the oppressed have cried for liberty, and a thousand man-made statutes have failed to give it to them. They can give it only to themselves; they shall find it only in obedience to the Divine Statutes which are inscribed upon their hearts. Let them resort to the inward Freedom, and the shadow of oppression shall no more darken the earth. Let men cease to oppress themselves, and no man shall oppress his brother.

Men legislate for an *outward* freedom, yet continue to render such freedom impossible of achievement by fostering an inward condition of enslavement. They thus pursue a shadow without, and ignore the substance within. Man will be free when he is freed from self. All outward forms of bondage and oppression will cease to be when man ceases to be the willing bond-slave of passion, error, and ignorance. Freedom is to the free.

While men cling to weakness they cannot have strength; while they love darkness they can receive no light; and so long as they prefer bondage they can enjoy no liberty. Strength, light, and freedom are ready now, and can be had by all who love them, who aspire to them. Freedom does not reside in cooperative aggression, for this will always produce, reactively, cooperative defense—hence warfare, hatred, party strife, and the destruction of liberty. Freedom resides in individual self-conquest. The emancipation of Humanity is frustrated and withheld by the self-enslavement of the unit. Thou who criest to man and God for liberty, liberate thyself!

The Heavenly Freedom is freedom from passion, from cravings, from opinions, from the tyranny of the flesh, and the tyranny of the intellect—this first, and then all outward freedom, as effect to cause. The Freedom that begins within, and extends outwardly until it embraces the whole man, is an emancipation so complete, all-embracing, and perfect as to leave no galling fetter unbroken. Free thy soul from all sin, and thou shalt walk a freed and fearless man in the midst of a world of fearful slaves; and, seeing thee, many slaves shall take heart and shall join thee in thy glorious freedom.

He who says, "My worldly duties are irksome to me; I will leave them and go into solitude, where I shall be as free as the air," and thinks to gain freedom thus, will find only a harder slavery. The tree of Freedom is rooted in Duty, and he who would pluck its sweet fruits must discover joy in Duty.

Glad-hearted, calm and ready for all tasks is he who is freed from self. Irksomeness and weariness cannot enter his heart, and his divine strength lightens every burden so that its weight is not felt. He does not run away from Duty with his chains about him, but breaks them and stands free.

Make thyself pure; make thyself proof against weakness, temptation, and sin; for only in thine own heart and mind shalt thou find that Perfect Freedom for which the whole world sighs and seeks in vain.

Greatness
and Goodness

Goodness, simplicity, greatness—these three are one, and this trinity of perfection cannot be separated. All greatness springs from goodness, and all goodness is profoundly simple. Without goodness there is no greatness. Some men pass through the world as destructive forces, like the tornado or the avalanche, but they are not great; they are to greatness as the avalanche is to the mountain. The work of greatness is enduring and preservative, and not violent and destructive. The greatest souls are the most gentle.

Greatness is never obtrusive. It works in silence, seeking no recognition. This is why it is not easily perceived and recognized. Like the mountain, it towers up in its vastness, so that those in its immediate vicinity, who receive its shelter and shade, do not see it. Its sublime grandeur is only beheld as they recede from it. The great man is not seen by his contemporaries; the majesty of his form is only outlined by its recession in time. This is the awe and enchantment of distance. Men occupy themselves with the small things; their houses, trees, lands. Few contemplate the mountain at whose base they live, and fewer still essay to explore it. But in the distance these small things disappear, and then the solitary beauty of the mountain is perceived. Popularity, noisy obtrusiveness, and shallow show, these superficialities rapidly disappear, and leave behind no enduring mark; whereas greatness slowly emerges from obscurity, and endures forever.

Jewish Rabbi and rabble alike saw not the divine beauty of Jesus; they saw only an unlettered carpenter. To his acquaintances, Homer was only a blind beggar, but the centuries reveal him as Homer the immortal poet. Two hundred years after the farmer of Stratford (and all that is known of him) has disappeared, the *real* Shakespeare is discerned. All true genius is impersonal. It belongs not to the man through whom it is manifested; it belongs to all. It is a diffusion of pure Truth; the Light of Heaven descending on all mankind.

Every work of genius, in whatsoever department of art, is a symbolic manifestation of impersonal

Truth. It is universal, and finds a response in every heart in every age and race. Anything short of this is not genius, is not greatness. That work which defends a *religion* perishes; it is *religion* that lives. Theories about immortality fade away; immortal man endures; commentaries upon Truth come to the dust; Truth alone remains. That only is true in art which represents the True; that only is great in life which is universally and eternally true. And the True is the Good; the Good is the True.

Every immortal work springs from the Eternal Goodness in the human heart, and it is clothed with the sweet and unaffected simplicity of goodness. The greatest art is, like nature, *artless*. It knows no trick, no pose, no studied effort. There are no stage-tricks in Shakespeare; and he is the greatest of dramatists because he is the *simplest*. The critics, not understanding the wise simplicity of greatness, always condemn the loftiest work. They cannot discriminate between the *childish* and the *childlike*. The True, the Beautiful, the Great, is always child-like, and is perennially fresh and young.

The great man is always the good man; he is always simple. He draws from, nay, lives in, the inexhaustible fountain of divine Goodness within; he inhabits the Heavenly Places; communes with the vanished great ones; lives with the Invisible: he is inspired, and breathes the airs of Heaven.

He who would be great let him learn to be good. He will therefore become great by not seeking greatness. Aiming at greatness a man arrives at nothingness; aiming at nothingness he arrives at greatness. The desire to be great is an indication of littleness, of personal vanity and obtrusiveness. The willingness to disappear from gaze, the utter absence of self-aggrandizement is the witness of greatness.

Littleness seeks and loves authority. Greatness is never authoritative, and it thereby becomes the authority to which the after ages appeal. He who seeks, loses; he who is willing to lose wins all men. Be thy simple self, thy better self, thy impersonal self, and lo! thou art great! He who selfishly seeks authority shall succeed only in becoming a trembling apologist courting protection behind the back of acknowledged greatness. He who will become the servant of all men, desiring no personal authority, shall live as a man, and shall be called *great*. "Abide in the simple and noble regions of thy life, obey thy heart, and thou shalt reproduce the foreworld again." Forget thine own little self, and fall back upon the Universal self, and thou shalt reproduce, in living and enduring forms, a thousand beautiful experiences; thou shalt find within thyself that simple goodness which is greatness.

"It is as easy to be great as to be small," says Emerson; and he utters a profound truth. Forgetfulness of self is the whole of greatness, as it is the whole of goodness and happiness. In a fleeting moment of self-forgetfulness the smallest soul becomes great; extend that moment indefinitely, and there is a great soul, a great life. Cast away thy personality (thy petty cravings, vanities, and ambitions) as a worthless garment, and dwell in the loving, compassionate, selfless regions of thy soul, and thou art no longer small—thou art great.

Claiming personal authority, a man descends into littleness; practicing goodness, a man ascends into greatness. The presumptuousness of the small may, for a time, obscure the humility of the great, but it is at last swallowed up by it, as the noisy river is lost in the calm ocean.

The vulgarity of ignorance and the pride of learning must disappear. Their worthlessness is equal. They have no part in the Soul of Goodness. If thou wouldst do, thou must *be*. Thou shalt not mistake information for Knowledge; thou must know thyself as pure Knowledge. Thou shalt not confuse learning with Wisdom; thou must apprehend thyself as undefiled Wisdom.

Wouldst thou write a living book? Thou must first *live*; thou shalt draw around thee the mystic garment of a manifold experience, and shalt learn, in enjoyment and suffering, gladness and sorrow, conquest and defeat, that which no book and no teacher can teach thee. Thou shalt learn of life, of thy soul; thou shalt tread the Lonely Road, and shalt *become*; thou shalt *be*. Thou shalt then write thy book, and it shall live; it shall be more than a book. Let thy book first live in thee, then shalt thou live in thy book.

Wouldst thou carve a statue that shall captivate the ages, or paint a picture that shall endure? Thou shalt acquaint thyself with the divine Beauty within thee. Thou shalt comprehend and adore the Invisible Beauty; thou shalt know the Principles which are the soul of Form; thou shalt perceive the matchless symmetry and faultless proportions of Life, of Being, of the Universe; thus knowing the eternally True thou shalt carve or paint the indescribably Beautiful.

Wouldst thou produce an imperishable poem? Thou shalt first live thy poem; thou shalt think and act rhythmically; thou shalt find the never-failing source of inspiration in the loving places of thy heart. Then shall immortal lines flow from thee without effort, and, as the flowers of wood and field spontaneously spring, so shall beautiful thoughts grow up in thine heart and, enshrined in words as molds to their beauty, shall subdue the hearts of men.

Wouldst thou compose such music as shall gladden and uplift the world? Thou shalt adjust thy soul to the Heavenly Harmonies. Thou shalt know that thyself, that life and the universe is Music. Thou shalt touch the chords of Life. Thou shalt know that Music is everywhere; that it is the Heart of Being; then shalt thou hear with thy spiritual ear the Deathless Symphonies.

Wouldst thou preach the living Word? Thou shalt forgo thyself, and become that Word. Thou shalt know one thing—*that the human heart is good, is divine*; thou shalt live one thing—*Love*. Thou shalt love all, seeing no evil, thinking no evil, believing no evil; then, though thou speak but little, thy every act shall be a power, thy every word a precept. By thy pure thought, thy selfless deed, though it appear hidden, thou shalt preach, down the ages, to untold multitudes of aspiring souls.

To him who chooses Goodness, sacrificing all, is given that which is more than and includes all. He becomes the possessor of the Best, communes with the Highest, and enters the company of the Great.

The greatness that is flawless, rounded, and complete is above and beyond all art. It is Perfect Goodness in manifestation; therefore the greatest souls are always Teachers.

Heaven
in the Heart

The toil of life ceases when the heart is pure. When the mind is harmonized with the Divine Law the wheel of drudgery ceases to turn, and all work is transmuted into joyful activity. The pure-hearted are as the lilies of the field, which toil not, yet are fed and clothed from the abundant storehouse of the All-Good. But the lily is not lethargic; it is ceaselessly active, drawing nourishment from earth and air and sun. By the Divine Power immanent within it, it builds itself up, cell by cell, opening itself to the light, growing and expanding toward the perfect flower. So is it with those who, having yielded up self-will, have learned to cooperate with the Divine Will. They grow in grace, goodness, and beauty, freed from anxiety and without friction and toil. And they never work in vain; there is no waste action. Every thought, act, and thing done subserves the Divine Purpose, and adds to the sum-total of the world's happiness.

Heaven is in the heart. They will look for it in vain who look elsewhere. In no outward place will the soul find Heaven until it finds it within itself; for, wherever the soul goes, its thoughts and desires will go with it; and, howsoever beautiful may be its outward dwelling-place, if there is sin within, there will be darkness and gloom without, for sin always casts a dark shadow over the pathway of the soul—the shadow of sorrow.

This world is beautiful, transcendently and wonderfully beautiful. Its beauties and inspiring wonders cannot be numbered; yet, to the sin-sodden mind, it appears as a dark and joyless place. Where passion and self are, there is hell, and there are all the pains of hell; where Holiness and Love are, there is Heaven, and there are all the joys of Heaven.

Heaven is here. It is also everywhere. It is wherever there is a pure heart. The whole universe is abounding with joy, but the sin-bound heart can neither see, hear, nor partake of it. No one is, or can be, arbitrarily shut out from Heaven; each shuts himself out. Its Golden Gates are eternally ajar, but the selfish cannot find them; they mourn, yet see not; they cry, but hear not. Only to those

who turn their eyes to heavenly things, their ears
to heavenly sounds, are the happy Portals of the
Kingdom revealed, and they enter and are glad.

All life is gladness when the heart is right, when
it is attuned to the sweet chords of holy Love. Life
is Religion, Religion is life, and all is Joy and Gladness. The jarring notes of creeds and parties, the
black shadows of sin, let them pass away forever;
they cannot enter the Door of Life; they form no
part of Religion. Joy, Music, Beauty—these belong
to the True Order of things; they are of the texture
of the universe; of these is the divine Garment of
Life woven. Pure Religion is glad, not gloomy. It is
Light without darkness or shadow.

Despondency, disappointment, grief—these are
the reflex aspects of pleasurable excitement, self-
seeking, and desire. Give up the latter, and the former will forever disappear; then there remains the
perfect Bliss of Heaven.

Abounding and unalloyed Happiness is man's
true life; perfect Blessedness is his rightful portion;
and when he loses his false life and finds the true
he enters into the full possession of his Kingdom.
The Kingdom of Heaven is man's Home: and it is
here and now, it is in his own heart, and he is not
left without Guides, if he wills to find it. All man's
sorrows and sufferings are the result of his own
self-elected estrangement from the Divine Source,

the All-Good, the Father, the Heart of Love. Let
him return to his Home; his peace awaits him.

The Heavenly-hearted are without sorrow and
suffering, because they are without sin. What the
worldly-minded call *troubles* they regard as pleasant
tasks of Love and Wisdom. Troubles belong to hell;
they do not enter Heaven, This is so simple it should
not appear strange. If you have a trouble it is in your
own mind, and nowhere else; you make it, it is not
made for you; it is not in your task; it is not in that
outward thing. You are its creator, and it derives its
life from you only. Look upon all your difficulties
as lessons to be learned, as aids to spiritual growth,
and lo! they are difficulties no longer! This is one of
the Pathways up to Heaven.

To transmute everything into Happiness and Joy,
this is supremely the work and duty of the Heavenly-
minded man. To reduce everything to wretchedness
and deprivation is the process which the worldly-
minded unconsciously pursue. To live in Love is to
work in Joy. Love is the magic that transforms all
things into power and beauty. It brings plenty out
of poverty, power out of weakness, loveliness out of
deformity, sweetness out of bitterness, light out of
darkness, and produces all blissful conditions out
of its own substantial but indefinable essence.

He who loves can never want. The universe
belongs to Goodness, and it therefore belongs to

the good man. It can be possessed by all without stint or shrinking, for Goodness, and the abundance of Goodness (material, mental, and spiritual abundance), is inexhaustible. Think lovingly, speak lovingly, act lovingly, and your every need shall be supplied; you shall not walk in desert places, and no danger shall overtake you.

Love sees with faultless vision, judges true judgment, acts in wisdom. Look through the eyes of Love, and you shall see everywhere the Beautiful and True; judge with the mind of Love, and you shall err not, shall awake no wail of sorrow; act in the spirit of Love, and you shall strike undying harmonies upon the Harp of Life.

Make no compromise with self. Cease not to strive until your whole being is swallowed up in Love. To love all and always—this is the Heaven of heavens. "Let there be nothing within thee that is not very beautiful and very gentle, and then will there be nothing without thee that is not beautified and softened by the spell of thy presence." All that you do, let it be done in calm wisdom, and not from desire, impulse, or opinion; this is the Heavenly way of action.

Purify your thought-world until no stain is left, and you will ascend into Heaven while living in the body. You will then see the things of the outward world clothed in all beautiful forms. Having found the Divine Beauty within ourselves, it springs to life in every outward thing. To the beautified soul the world is beautiful.

Undeveloped souls are merely unopened flowers. The perfect Beauty lies concealed within, and will one day reveal itself to the full-orbed light of Heaven. Seeing men thus, we stand where evil is not, and where the eye beholds only good. Herein lies the peace and patience and beauty of Love— *it sees no evil.* He who loves thus becomes the protector of all men. Though in their ignorance they should hate him, he shields and loves them.

What gardener is so foolish as to condemn his flowers because they do not develop in a day? Learn to love, and you shall see in all souls, even those called "degraded," the Divine Beauty, and shall know that it will not fail to come forth in its own season. This is one of the Heavenly Visions; it is out of this that Gladness comes.

Sin, sorrow, suffering—these are the dark gropings of the unopened soul for Light. Open the petals of your soul and let the glorious Light stream in.

Every sinful soul is an unresolved harmony. It shall at last strike the Perfect Chord, and swell the joyful melodies of Heaven.

Hell is the preparation for Heaven; and out of the debris of its ruined hovels are built pleasant mansions wherein the perfected soul may dwell.

Night is only a fleeting shadow which the world casts, and sorrow is but a transient shade cast by the self. "Come out into the Sunlight." Know this, O reader! that you are divine. You are not cut off from the Divine except in your own unbelief. Rise up, O Son of God! and shake off the nightmare of sin which binds you; accept your heritage—the Kingdom of Heaven! Drug your soul no longer with the poisons of false beliefs. You are not "a worm of the dust" unless you choose to make yourself one. You are a divine, immortal, God-born being, and this you may know if you will to seek and find. Cling no longer to your impure and groveling thoughts, and you shall know that you are a radiant and celestial spirit, filled with all pure and lovable thoughts. Wretchedness and sin and sorrow are not your portion here unless you accept them as such; and if you do this, they will be your portion hereafter, for these things are not apart from your soulcondition; they will go wherever you go; they are only within you.

Heaven, not hell, is your portion here and always. It only requires you to take that which belongs to you. You are the master, and you choose whom you will serve. You are the maker of your state, and your choice determines your condition. What you pray and ask for (with your mind and heart, not with your lips merely), this you receive.

You are served as you serve. You are conditioned as you condition. You garner in your own.

Heaven is yours; you have but to enter in and take possession; and Heaven means Supreme Happiness, Perfect Blessedness; it leaves nothing to be desired; nothing to be grieved over. It is complete satisfaction *now and in this world*. It is within you; and if you do not know this, it is because you persist in turning the back of your soul upon it. *Turn round* and you shall behold it.

Come and live in the sunshine of your being. Come out of the shadows and the dark places. You are framed for Happiness. You are a child of Heaven. Purity, Wisdom, Love, Plenty, Joy, and Peace—these are the eternal Realities of the Kingdom, and they are yours, but you cannot possess them in sin; they have no part in the Realm of Darkness. They belong to "the Light which lighteth every man that cometh into the world," the Light of spotless Love. They are the heritage of the holy Christ-Child who shall come to birth in your soul when you are ready to divest yourself of all your impurities. They are your real self.

But he whose soul has been safely delivered of the Wonderful Joy-Child does not forget the travail of the world.

James Allen: A Memoir

By Lily L. Allen
from *The Epoch* (February–March 1912)

> *Unto pure devotion*
> *Devote thyself: with perfect meditation*
> *Comes perfect act, and the right-hearted rise—*
> *More certainly because they seek no gain—*
> *Forth from the bands of body, step by step.*
> *To highest seats of bliss.*

James Allen was born in Leicester, England, on November 28th, 1864. His father, at one time a very prosperous manufacturer, was especially fond of "Jim," and before great financial failures overtook him, he would often look at the delicate, refined boy, poring over his books, and would say, "My boy, I'll make a scholar of you."

The Father was a high type of man intellectually, and a great reader, so could appreciate the evident thirst for education and knowledge which he observed in his quiet studious boy.

As a young child he was very delicate and nervous, often suffering untold agony during his school days through the misunderstanding harshness of some of his school teachers, and others with whom he was forced to associate, though he retained always the tenderest memories of others—one or two of his teachers in particular, who no doubt are still living.

He loved to get alone with his books, and many a time he has drawn a vivid picture for me, of the hours he spent with his precious books in his favourite corner by the home fire; his father, whom he dearly loved, in his arm chair opposite also deeply engrossed in his favourite authors. On such evenings he would question his father on some of the profound thoughts that surged through his soul—thoughts he could scarcely form into words—and the father, unable to answer, would gaze at him long over his spectacles, and at last say: "My boy, my boy, you have lived before"—and when the boy eagerly but reverently would suggest an answer to his own question, the father would grow silent and thoughtful, as though he *sensed* the future man and his mission, as he looked at the boy and listened to his words—and many a time he was heard to remark, "Such knowledge comes not in one short life."

There were times when the boy startled those about him into a deep concern for his health, and they would beg him not to *think so much*, and in after years he often smiled when he recalled how his father would say—"Jim, we will have you in the Churchyard soon, if you think so much."

Not that he was by any means unlike other boys where games were concerned. He could play leap-frog and marbles with the best of them, and those who knew him as a man—those who were privileged to meet him at "Bryngoleu"—will remember how he could enter into a game with all his heart. Badminton he delighted in during the summer evenings, or whenever he felt he could.

About three years after our marriage, when our little Nora was about eighteen months old, and he about thirty-three, I realized a great change coming over him, and knew that he was renouncing everything that most men hold dear that he might find Truth, and lead the weary sin-stricken world to Peace. He at that time commenced the practice of rising early in the morning, at times long before daylight, that he might go out on the hills—like One of old—to commune with God, and meditate on Divine things. I do not claim to have understood him fully in those days. The light in which he lived and moved was far too white for my earth-bound eyes to see, and a *sense of it only* was beginning to dawn upon me. But I knew I dare not stay him or hold him back, though at times my woman's heart cried out to do so, waiting him all my own, and not then understanding his divine mission.

Then came his first book, "From Poverty to Power." This book is considered by many his best book. It has passed into many editions, and tens of thousands have been sold all over the world, both authorized and pirated editions, for perhaps no author's works have been more pirated than those of James Allen.

As a private secretary he worked from 9 a.m. to 6 p.m., and used every moment out of office writing his books. Soon after the publication of "From Poverty to Power" came "All These Things Added," and then "As a Man Thinketh," a book perhaps better known and more widely read than any other from his pen.

About this time, too, the "Light of Reason" was founded and he gave up all his time to the work of editing the Magazine, at the same time carrying on a voluminous correspondence with searchers after Truth all over the world. And ever as the years went by he kept straight on, and never once looked back or swerved from the path of holiness. Oh, it was a blessed thing indeed to be the chosen one to walk by the side of his earthly body, and to watch the glory dawning upon him!

He took a keen interest in many scientific subjects, and always eagerly read the latest discovery in astronomy, and he delighted in geology and botany. Among his favourite books I find Shakespeare, Milton, Emerson, Browning, The Bhagavad-Gita, the Tao-Tea-King of Lao-Tze, the Light of Asia, the Gospel of Buddha, Walt Whitman, Dr. Bucke's Cosmic Consciousness, and the Holy Bible.

He might have written on a wide range of subjects had he chosen to do so, and was often asked for articles on many questions outside his particular work, but he refused to comply, consecrating his whole thought and effort to preach the Gospel of Peace.

When physical suffering overtook him he never once complained, but grandly and patiently bore his pain, hiding it from those around him, and only we who knew and loved him so well, and his kind, tender Doctor, knew how greatly he suffered. And yet he stayed not; still he rose before the dawn to meditate, and commune with God; still he sat at his desk and wrote those words of Light and Life which will ring down through the ages, calling men and women from their sins and sorrows to peace and rest.

Always strong in his complete manhood, though small of stature physically, and as gentle as he was strong, no one ever heard an angry word from those kind lips. Those who served him adored him; those who had business dealings with him trusted and honoured him. Ah! how much my heart prompts me to write of his self-sacrificing life, his tender words, his gentle deeds, his knowledge and his wisdom. But why? Surely there is no need, for do not his books speak in words written by his own hand, and will they not speak to generations yet to come?

About Christmas time I saw the change coming, and understood it not—blind! blind! blind! I could not think it possible that *he* should be taken and *I* left.

But we three—as if we knew—clung closer to each other, and loved one another with a greater love—if that were possible—than ever before. Look at his portrait given with the January "Epoch," and reproduced again in this, and you will see that even then our Beloved, our Teacher and Guide, was letting go his hold on the physical. He was leaving us then, and we didn't know it. Often I had urged him to stop work awhile and rest, but he always gave me the same answer, "My darling, when I stop I must go, don't try to stay my hand."

And so he worked on, until that day, Friday, January 12, 1912, when, about one o'clock he sat down in his chair, and looking at me with a great compassion and yearning in those blessed eyes, he cried out, as he stretched out his arms to me, *"Oh, I have finished, I have finished, I can go no further, I have done."*

Need I say that everything that human aid and human skill could do was done to keep him still with us. Of those last few days I dare scarcely write. How could my pen describe them? And when we knew the end was near, with his dear hands upon my head in blessing, he gave his work and his beloved people into my hands, charging me to bless and help them, until I received the call to give up my stewardship!

"I will help you," he said, "and if I can I shall come to you and be with you often."

Words, blessed words of love and comfort, *for my heart alone* often came from his lips, and a sweet smile ever came over the pale calm face when our little Nora came to kiss him and speak loving words to him, while always the gentle voice breathed the tender words to her—*"My little darling!"*

So calmly, peacefully, quietly, he passed from us at the dawn on Wednesday, January 24, 1912. "Passed from us," did I say? Nay, only the outer garment has passed from our mortal vision. He lives! and when the great grief that tears our hearts at the separation is calmed and stilled, I think that we shall know that he is still with us. We shall again rejoice in his companionship and presence.

When his voice was growing faint and low, I heard him whispering, and leaning down to catch the words I heard—"At last, at last—at home—my wanderings are over"—and then, I heard no more, for my heart was breaking within me, and I felt, for *him* indeed it was "*Home at last!*" but for me—And then, as though he knew my thoughts, he turned and again holding out his hands to me, he said: "I have only one thing more to say to you, my beloved, and that is I love you, and I will be waiting for you; good-bye."

I write this memoir for those who love him, for those who will read it with tender loving hearts, and tearful eyes; for those who will not look critically at the way in which I have tried to tell out of my lonely heart this short story of his life and passing away—for *his* pupils, and, therefore, my friends.

We clothed the mortal remains in *pure white linen*, symbol of his fair, pure life, and so, clasping the photo of the one he loved best upon his bosom—they committed all that remained to the funeral pyre.

About the Author

James Allen was one of the pioneering figures of the self-help movement and modern inspirational thought. A philosophical writer and poet, he is best known for his book *As a Man Thinketh*. Writing about complex subjects such as faith, destiny, love, patience, and religion, he had the unique ability to explain them in a way that is simple and easy to comprehend. He often wrote about cause and effect, as well as overcoming sadness, sorrow and grief.

Allen was born in 1864 in Leicester, England into a working-class family. His father travelled alone to America to find work, but was murdered within days of arriving. With the family now facing economic disaster, Allen, at age 15, was forced to leave school and find work to support them.

During stints as a private secretary and stationer, he found that he could showcase his spiritual and social interests in journalism by writing for the magazine *The Herald of the Golden Age.*

In 1901, when he was 37, Allen published his first book, *From Poverty to Power.* In 1902 he began to publish his own spiritual magazine, *The Light of Reason* (which would be retitled *The Epoch* after his death). Each issue contained announcements, an editorial written by Allen on a different subject each month, and many articles, poems, and quotes written by popular authors of the day and even local, unheard of authors.

His third and most famous book *As a Man Thinketh* was published in 1903. The book's minor popularity enabled him to quit his secretarial work and pursue his writing and editing career full time. He wrote 19 books in all, publishing at least one per year while continuing to publish his magazine, until his death. Allen wrote when he had a message—one that he had lived out in his own life and knew that it was good.

In 1905, Allen organized his magazine subscribers into groups (called "The Brotherhood") that would meet regularly and reported on their meetings each month in the magazine. Allen and his wife, Lily Louisa Oram, whom he had married in 1895, would often travel to these group meetings to give speeches and read articles. Some of Allen's favorite writings, and those he quoted often, include the works of Shakespeare, Milton, Emerson, the Bible, Buddha, Whitman, Trine, and Lao-Tze.

Allen died in 1912 at the age of 47. Following his death, Lily, with the help of their daughter, Nora took over the editing of *The Light of Reason*, now under the name *The Epoch*. Lily continued to publish the magazine until her failing eyesight prevented her from doing so. Lily's life was devoted to spreading the works of her husband until her death at age 84.

CPSIA information can be obtained
at www.ICGtesting.com
Printed in the USA
BVHW070942170719
553679BV00012B/78/P

9 781722 502485